Elite • 245

The Dutch Resistance 1940–45

World War II Resistance and Collaboration in the Netherlands

**MICHEL WENTING LLM &
KLAAS CASTELEIN**

ILLUSTRATED BY MARK STACEY

Series editors Martin Windrow & Nick Reynolds

OSPREY PUBLISHING
Bloomsbury Publishing Plc
Kemp House, Chawley Park, Cumnor Hill, Oxford OX2 9PH, UK
29 Earlsfort Terrace, Dublin 2, Ireland
1385 Broadway, Fifth Floor, New York, NY 10018, USA
E-mail: info@ospreypublishing.com
www.ospreypublishing.com

OSPREY is a trademark of Osprey Publishing Ltd

First published in Great Britain in 2022

© Osprey Publishing Ltd 2022

A catalogue record for this book is available from the British Library

ISBN: PB 9781472848024; eBook: 9781472848000; ePDF: 9781472847997;
XML:9781472847980

Editor: Martin Windrow
Index by Zoe Ross
Typeset by PDQ Digital Media Solutions, Bungay, UK
Printed and bound in India by Replika Press Private Ltd

Osprey Publishing supports the Woodland Trust, the UK's leading woodland conservation charity.

To find out more about our authors and books, visit
www.ospreypublishing.com. Here you will find extracts, author interviews, details of forthcoming events, and the option to sign up for our newsletter.

DEDICATION

The authors would like to dedicate this book to all those who contributed to opposing the Nazi regime in one way or another, in particular: Dominicus Ettema; Antoon Helmes (great-uncle of Michel Wenting) and his wife Leopoldine Johanna 'Poldi' Gebauer; Hielke Brouwer and Gelske Brouwer-de Boer (great-grandparents of Klaas Castelein); Klaas van der Meer (grandfather of Klaas Castelein); and Karel de Smalen (uncle of Klaas Castelein).

Mr Ettema and Mr Helmes were friends who founded the National Organization (LO) branch in Bergh, a municipality in the eastern province of Gelderland. Mr Ettema died on 11 January 1945 in Neuengamme concentration camp. Subsequently Mr Helmes became the commander of the Netherlands Interior Forces (NBS) group at Zeddam, a village in Bergh municipality. His wife Mrs Gebauer supported him in his Resistance work. Mr Brouwer headed the LO branch in Achtkarspelen, a municipality in the northern province of Friesland. He and his wife Mrs Brouwer-De Boer were later recognized by Yad Vashem for having aided persecuted Jews in hiding. In addition, Mr Brouwer became a commander in the NBS group in Achtkarspelen. Mr Van der Meer escorted Jewish fugitives between hiding-places, and delivered food coupons to Jews and railway strikers in hiding. At the tender age of around ten years, Mr De Smalen distributed *Trouw* ('Loyal'), an underground Protestant newspaper, in Amsterdam.

EDITOR'S NOTE

Throughout this text modern Dutch spelling is used, which differs in some cases from that used in wartime: e.g., modern *'Germaanse'* for wartime *'Germaansche', 'Nederlandse'* for *'Nederlandsche',* and *'Stoter'* for *'Stooter'.* To avoid a confusing amount of italics in some passages, only Dutch and occasional French and Frisian words are italicized, but not German.

ACKNOWLEDGEMENTS

to persons and institutions: Böcker, Ernst-August, owner of a photograph showing German Wachmänner; Braam, Conny, expert on the Dutch Resistance in IJmuiden, Velsen and Haarlem; Bruggink, Jan, expert on Drenthe province during World War II; Heuvel, Constant van den, expert on Veenendaal municipality during World War II; Keizer, Jasper, expert on Friesland province during World War II; Mulder, Gerard, expert on the Dutch Resistance in the Veluwe; Vrolings, Gaston, expert on militaria and fascism in the Netherlands.

Museum Rotterdam; National Military Museum (NMM); Netherlands Institute for Military History (NIMH); Tresoar.

Title page photo

25 September 1944, Eindhoven area of North Brabant province: a PAN member named Jan Vlaswinkel guiding follow-on troops of British XXX Corps near the town of Valkenswaard. He wears the brassard illustrated as Plate H5, and carries a semi-automatic pistol. Although this photo taken late in Operation *Market Garden* has a staged appearance, it accurately depicts one of the most valuable roles of the Resistance during the Allied advances. (Imperial War Museum, London)

CONTENTS

Parade by paramilitaries of the *NSNAP-Rappard* faction, probably during 1941. The uniforms appear virtually identical to those of the German Nazi Party's SA 'stormtroopers', and note the SA dagger – see Plate A3. While this faction's ideology was more closely aligned with that of the Nazi Party, the wider support base and better organization of Mussert's *Nationaal-Socialistische Beweging* (NSB) made that movement more attractive to the German authorities as a partner for practical cooperation. (Courtesy Gaston Vrolings)

Initially the German administration had been foreseen as purely military; however, as early as 17 May 1940, Hitler ordered its subordination to a political authority. Supreme executive power was vested in a Reichskommissar (governor), an Austrian Nazi named Arthur Seyss-Inquart. The former Dutch government's administrative organization was almost entirely retained, under the direction and supervision of this Reich Commissioner and four subordinate General Commissioners.

Ground forces

Over time Gen Christiansen's military forces varied in strength, from about 50,000–60,000 in early 1942 to some 125,000 in late 1943. Although this total included both active formations and training units of the Replacement Army, such figures in themselves posed a formidable obstacle to the initiation and sustaining of Dutch armed resistance.

In June 1944, at the time of the Allied landings in Normandy, the Netherlands garrison under Heeresgruppe B comprised four divisions (347. & 719. Inf Divs, 16. Luftwaffe Field Div, and 19. Panzer Division). On 4 September 1944, Gen Kurt Student's First Parachute Army, with seven divisions (although only 6. Fallschirm Div was even nominally an airborne formation), reinforced Army Group B in the Netherlands, where the post-Normandy remnants of SS-Gruppenführer Wilhelm Bittrich's II SS-Panzer Corps were already refitting. Following the subsequent Allied liberation of North Brabant and Limburg provinces, on 11 November 1944 Army Group H was formed under Gen Student to defend the rest of the Netherlands with Fifteenth and First Parachute armies, and other remaining garrison units were formed into a weak three-division Twenty-Fifth Army under operational command of Gen Christiansen's chief-of-staff, Gen von Wülisch.

Rare photo of the short-lived *Grauwe Vendels* paramilitaries of the *Nationaal Front* during a flag-raising ceremony in summer 1940; members were only allowed to wear uniform when on duty. During research for this book the authors were unable to identify a specific flag design for the NF, but most Dutch fascists favoured the old orange/ white/ blue colours associated with 16th-century Dutch insurgents. (Beeldbankwo2.nl/ Netherlands Institute for War Documentation, NIOD)

Luftwaffe

In July 1940 the Air Force initially deployed the headquarters and some bomber units of IX Fliegerdivision in the Netherlands to strike at Great Britain, alongside the rest of Luftflotten 2 and 3 based in Belgium and northern France. Within a year, after failure in the Battle of Britain, the Luftwaffe's role there became largely defensive. The Netherlands became the first line of Germany's western air defence for its industrial heartland in the Ruhr area (roughly, bounded by the Rhine, Lippe and Ruhr rivers). To counter the British Royal Air Force's initially feeble but steadily growing bomber threat, extensive searchlight and anti-aircraft artillery batteries, sound detection installations, and soon a sophisticated chain of radar stations were installed, and the first German night fighters operated from Dutch airfields. The ensuing air war over the Netherlands would eventually cost the lives of almost 20,000 Allied and German airmen, and the destruction of some 6,000 aircraft.

Kriegsmarine

In May 1940, 22 ships of the Royal Dutch Navy fell into German hands, and were subsequently used by the Kriegsmarine (though only a handful of Dutch nationals served in the German Navy), and during the war German naval recruits received training in the Netherlands. In addition to regular deployments of Schnellboote (motor torpedo boats) along the coast, some 'Biber' midget submarines operated from Rotterdam in December 1944– April 1945. During the Occupation the Dutch ship-building industry was also absorbed into the German war effort.

While showing GV men performing the more mundane task of repairing a bicycle tyre, this does reveal a few more details of the uniform, which we reconstruct as Plate A2. Taken in June 1941, it also confirms that the GV continued to appear in uniform well after their official disbandment in October 1940. The man on the left is Sjef Paijmans, a hussar unit veteran of the May 1940 campaign who joined the NF and the GV after the Dutch capitulation. Following the 1945 liberation he was severely mistreated while interned at Vught alongside Dutch SS-men. (Courtesy Joost Paijmans)

PARAMILITARY ORGANIZATIONS

The German authorities raised a number of paramilitary organizations in order to bolster their war effort – too many to mention all of them here, but the following were the most relevant.

Organization Todt (OT)

From 1943 onwards some German troops under the supervision of the Organization Todt, a German paramilitary construction conglomerate – (see MAA 254, *Wehrmacht Auxiliary Forces)* – worked on the Atlantikwall. This series of coastal fortifications stretched from Norway all the way down to the French-Spanish border, being designed to repel any potential Allied invasion. The consequent uprooting of Dutch civilian coastal communities caused anti-German feeling, though not so much as did the conscription of many thousands of Dutch forced labourers to work on these defences. Later, lines of defence in the interior were also established, updating the OT's pre-war Westwall – which ran from the Dutch–German border down to Switzerland – into what the Allies would call the 'Siegfried Line'.

A security wing of the OT was known as Schutzkommando-OT (SK-OT). Its main responsibility was to maintain discipline and order among the non-German workers, as well as guarding OT construction camps and other installations against hostile activities and theft. The SK-OT guards were

B

LABOUR SERVICES, & STATE POLICE

(1) *Arbeidsman, Nederlandse Arbeidsdienst*, 1940–45

NAD members wore 'bronze-green' uniforms, most of them from re-dyed former Dutch Army stocks. The M31 sidecaps, overcoats, tunics, trousers and puttees were made from woollen cloth all dyed the same colour. The cap bore either a Dutch cockade, or the NAD badge (see **1a**) in golden-yellow on burgundy-red. For this basic rank of 'Worker' the tunic's rectangular burgundy collar patches bore crossed heads of barley embroidered in 'gold' wire. A leather belt, and blackened former Dutch Army hobnailed ankle boots, were worn with the uniform. On parade, this *Arbeidsman* stands to attention and 'presents' his spade in salute.

(1a) NAD cap badge

The BeVo-woven NAD emblem consisted of a golden-yellow spade between two heads of barley, on a burgundy-red shield. The motto reads *Ick dien* ('I serve').

(2) Vormann, RAD Oostkorps; Russia, 1942–44

This Dutch volunteer for the Reichsarbeitsdienst, working behind the Eastern Front, wears RAD uniform; this was usually drab greyish-brown, but sometimes of a greener shade. On the dark brown collar he displays second-pattern patches for this rank: black, with pointed white braids bearing a single grey line. The plain shoulder straps are piped infantry-white. Above his Nazi Party brassard is a shield-shaped national patch striped orange/ white/ blue, with black lettering 'Nederland' on the central white stripe. Given the hazards of service in often thinly-guarded rear areas, the volunteers were armed, in this case with a former Czech 7.92mm Mauser vz. rifle (German designation Gewehr 24). They also received German steel helmets with Army decals, and personal field equipment. This 'Foreman' carries the felt-covered canteen with its black bakelite cup hooked to his canvas bread-bag (haversack), all attached, with a spade, to the bicycle's cord-wrapped handlebars.

(3) *Wachtmeester, Staatspolitie*; Schalkhaar, February 1944

Our figure is based on a *Staatspolitie* officer (and war criminal) named Dirk Hoogendam, who appears on film taken during a visit by Himmler on 1 February 1944 to the Police Training Battalion at Schalkhaar near Deventer and the SS School 'Avegoor' in the village of Ellecom, near Arnhem. From the end of November 1944, Hoogendam would command a company of the *Landstorm Nederland* (see below), which hunted down Resistance fighters and other fugitives in the provinces of Gelderland, Overijssel and Drenthe.

The new uniform and the introduction of military-style ranks are a clear expression of the 'Nazification' of the Dutch police. This is most evident in the cap, which obviously copies the German high-fronted Schirmmütze. Royal-blue piping at the crown seam and top and bottom of the band is hardly visible here against the black cloth. The white-metal upper badge depicts a flaming 'grenade' (actually, a shell); below it, an oval cockade in the Dutch national colours (red/ white/ blue centre) is surrounded by an oakleaf wreath. The four-pocket black tunic has seven white-metal front buttons, all buttons on the uniform showing the flaming-grenade emblem. Note the 'scooped' chevron of royal-blue piping above each cuff; the plaited royal-blue shoulder cords; and the royal-blue patches on the stand-and-fall collar, displaying the single vertical yellow stripe of sergeant's rank.

The various awards on Hoogendam's chest show that prior to joining the State Police he was a Waffen-SS combat veteran of the Eastern Front, probably in SS-PzGren Regt 10 'Westland' of the SS-PzGren Div 'Wiking'. Between the front buttons he sports the ribbon of the Iron Cross 2nd Class. On his pocket, from left to right, are the silver Infantry Assault Badge; a Wound Badge also in silver (for three or four wounds); and white-embroidered SS runes. This last indicates that he was also a member of the single SS-Polizei Standarte (SS Police Regt) among the six regiments of the *Germaanse-SS in Nederland*.

1

1a

2

3

ICK DIEN

armed, and received full military training. They wore the brown OT uniform with black shoulder straps piped infantry-white, and had their own rank insignia. Several Dutchmen serving in the SK-OT guarded their fellow countrymen employed as forced labourers.

Nederlandse Arbeidsdienst (NAD, Netherlands Labour Service)

On 15 October 1940 the German authorities established the Netherlands Labour Service, which was clearly modelled on Germany's Reichsarbeitsdienst (RAD, Reich Labour Service – again, see MAA 254). The NAD's main tasks were clearing land, forestry, earth-moving and agriculture. The Germans encouraged NAD members who had served their time to enlist for Waffen-SS or other military service.

Initially the NAD was formed with volunteers, but on 1 April 1942 it was made compulsory for all young Dutchmen aged 18 to 23 years. From that date onwards, certain categories within that age group would be

Nederlandse Arbeidsdienst labourer; compare with Plate B1 & B1a. The sidecap might bear either the shield-shaped NAD badge or, as here, a red/ white/ blue-centred Dutch cockade. Note the burgundy-red collar patches with crossed heads of barley embroidered in gold-coloured wire. (Beeldbankwo2. nl/ NIOD)

called up for labour service as needed. Shortly after 5 September 1944, when it seemed that the Netherlands would be liberated within a few days, almost all NAD labourers deserted their camps throughout the country, and three-quarters of the NAD leadership also disappeared. The remainder were absorbed into the RAD, and used mainly to build defences in the eastern and northern provinces of the Netherlands.

Oostkorps (RAD East Corps)

From the beginning of 1942, workers were also recruited to enlist for service, often under OT supervision, behind the Eastern Front in the Gruppe Niederlande im Reichsarbeitsdienst ('Netherlands Group in the Reich Labour Service'). Many hundreds of NAD members volunteered for what was popularly known as the *Oostkorps*. This service was not without its dangers, due to the continuous threats posed by Soviet and Polish partisans in the Wehrmacht's huge and sparsely guarded rear areas in the East. For this reason these volunteers were trained and armed, in most cases with captured weapons, and some would become casualties during clashes with partisans. When the general advances by the Soviet armies began in 1943–44, the East Corps units were gradually withdrawn to the Netherlands. Those who had completed their contracted service in the East were permitted to wear on the left forearm a maroon-red cuff title with the white woven lettering 'OOSTKORPS'.

THE SECURITY APPARATUS

General Commission for Security

On Reichskommissar Seyss-Inquart's staff, the Generalkommissar für das Sicherheitswesen und Höhere SS- und Polizeiführer ('General Commissioner for Security, and Higher SS and Police Commander' – HSSPF) was a fellow Austrian, SS-Gruppenführer (lieutenant-general, SS-Gruf) Hanns Albin Rauter. A veteran of the Austrian mountain troops in World War I, and later of the Bavarian Freikorps Oberland in Upper Silesia in 1921, Rauter had joined the SS in Germany in 1935. Although formally subordinate to Seyss-Inquart, Rauter also took orders directly from Reichsführer-SS Himmler in Berlin, and was his *de facto* plenipotentiary in the Netherlands.[1]

Rauter had under his command all SS and German police garrison units stationed in the country, including: the military Waffen-SS; the political Allgemeine-SS; the Sicherheitspolizei (Sipo) Security Police, and its subsidiary Secret State Police (Gestapo); the Sicherheitsdienst (SD) SS Security Service; and the Ordnungspolizei (Orpo) Order Police – the latter known as 'Green Police', since their uniform colour differed from the Army's 'field-grey'. As well as Germans, some Dutchmen served individually in these security branches, fighting actively against the Resistance.

Parading Dutch volunteer *Oostkorps* labourer serving with the German RAD behind the Russian Front – compare with Plate B2. He wears an M35 German helmet complete with the Army decal, and RAD uniform with a 'Nederland' left sleeve shield replacing the RAD's usual 'spade-head' badge bearing battalion and company numbers. However, like German RAD personnel, he also displays the Nazi Party brassard. (Walburg Pers)

1 During the reaction to Operation *Market Garden* in September 1944, Rauter would briefly command a battle-group, bringing him excessively generous promotion to SS-Obergruppenführer (general, SS-Ogruf) und General der Waffen-SS. Deployed north of Arnhem, Kampfgruppe Rauter consisted of the *Landstorm Nederland*, SS-Wachbataillon Nordwest, and a Polizei regiment.

Plain-clothes security agents examining the identity documents of Jewish citizens in Amsterdam in the summer of 1942; note the compulsory yellow star badge. In May 1940 the Jewish community in the Netherlands had numbered about 140,000 people. Of those, some 101,800 would die during the Holocaust, either murdered in the extermination camps or dying of disease, hunger and exhaustion. (Beeldbankwo2. nl/ NIOD)

A group of Wachmänner recruited from among German nationals already living in the Netherlands. The owner of this photograph (whose father, Ernst Böcker, is second from left), confirms that they wear green-dyed ex-Dutch Army uniforms – see Plate C2. Only the man at far right wears puttees, the others boots or gaiters. These Watchmen were tasked with guarding various canal bridges between Dieren and Apeldoorn in Gelderland province. (Courtesy Ernst-August Böcker)

After the liberation of Belgium and the southern part of the Netherlands in September 1944, some French and Belgian members of the SD also found a temporary refuge in the still-occupied northern Dutch provinces. (Although popularly referred to as 'Rexists', in fact most Belgian SD men were Flemish fascists rather than members of Léon Degrelle's Rexist Party, which drew its support from Wallonia, the Francophone southern part of Belgium.) Some other members were ethnic Germans from Poland, Ukraine, Czechoslovakia and Romania. These SD units, regarded as the bloodhounds of the Nazi authorities, fought viciously against the Dutch Resistance until the very end of the war, gaining a notorious reputation among the civil population.

The main SS-run detention, concentration and transit camps established in the Netherlands were at Westerbork in Drenthe province (where

SS-Gruppenführer Rauter (centre, speaking to a trainee), HSSPF in the occupied Netherlands, photographed on 26 February 1942 during an inspection visit to the *Staatspolitie* Training Battalion at Schalkhaar. To our left of Rauter stands SS-Brigadeführer und Generalmajor der Polizei Otto Schumann. Between Rauter and the trainee is the NSB leader Leo Broersen, *Staatspolitie* chief-of-staff; under a leather coat, he wears the black uniform of the *Nederlandse-SS* (soon to be renamed the *Germaanse-SS in Nederland*), with cap badges of the NSB *wolfsangel* above the SS death's-head. (Beeldbankwo2.nl/ NIOD)

Jewish deportees were assembled), Ommen in Overijssel, Amersfoort in Utrecht, and a cluster in and around Vught in North Brabant. Additionally, a new wing for political prisoners was opened at Scheveningen prison in that suburb of The Hague.

In the initial stage of the Occupation the German authorities sought to win the 'hearts and minds' of the Dutch people, hoping that in time they could be persuaded to identify themselves as members of the 'greater Germanic race' and to ally themselves with the Third Reich. To this end the Germans granted a major concession: the quick release of almost all Dutch prisoners of war of the May 1940 campaign, in stark contrast to the continued captivity of French PoWs.

General Christiansen also sought to distance his soldiers from the harsher security measures, but the Army's early reputation among the Dutch for 'correct' behaviour did not last long. After the February 1941 strike in protest at the first arrests of Dutch Jews (see below), and as the German authorities thereafter stepped up their repressive measures, the Army was inevitably drawn into providing support for Rauter's round-ups of Jews and other fugitives, and the shooting of Dutch hostages.

One of very few known photos of the Kontroll-Kommando, showing a guard at Camp Erika, Ommen – see Plate C1. His Dutch Army M12 sidecap displays a woven SS death's-head badge, but no eagle-and-swastika; the white letters 'K.K.' can just be made out on his right collar patch. (Beeldbankwo2.nl/ NIOD)

A major provocation, on 29 April 1943, was a decree that former Dutch PoWs should report for registration – in practice, for the forced labour known as Arbeitseinsatz (in Dutch, *arbeidsinzet*), which often involved deportation to Germany. Over the following two years the Germans also subjected the population to widespread requisitions of anything deemed of value: radios, trams, boats, bicycles, farm livestock, even textiles. These depredations, alongside increasingly violent acts of repression, naturally hardened Dutch hatred of their occupiers as every day passed.

LOCAL SECURITY FORCES
Nazification of the Dutch police

In May 1940 the Dutch police force was about 13,000 strong, divided between the *Koninklijke Marechaussee*, the *Rijksveldwacht* (Gendarmerie), the *Gemeentepolitie* (Municipal Police) and the *Gemeenteveldwacht* (Municipal Gendarmerie). During the Occupation the *Marechaussee* lost its designation *Koninklijke* ('Royal'), and was essentially absorbed into the civil police.[2] Under the HSSPF's reforms the entire Dutch police, from the highest to the lowest echelons, came under the strict supervision of the Orpo.

The police officers who remained in service during the Occupation found themselves in a difficult position, being required to arrest Jews, Resistance

2 The term *Marechaussee* is often inadequately translated as 'military police'. Until 1939 this branch was a militarized corps with civilian police duties. During the 1939-40 mobilization it was a military corps with military tasks. Thereafter, during the Occupation it was exclusively employed as a civilian police corps.

members, shot-down Allied airmen, escaped PoWs, and, from spring 1943, people hiding to evade forced labour. Many police officers did not sympathize with the Germans, but nevertheless continued to serve for various reasons (most understandably, simply in order to be able to feed their families). It is estimated that about ten per cent of Dutch police officers were involved in the Resistance in one way or another, but this was a tricky path to follow. For instance, a policeman could not warn the Resistance of every imminent round-up, since this would quickly attract German suspicion and identification. Thus, policemen had to navigate an ethical minefield as to when or not to warn people in danger.

After the surrender and disarmament of the Dutch Army in May 1940, the police were the only armed and uniformed force tolerated by the German authorities. Rauter's security apparatus set about 'Nazifying' the Dutch police, upon whose obedient cooperation it was dependent to implement its repressive programme. In 1941, in order to cultivate a new crop of reliable police officers to be called the *Staatspolitie* (State Police), two training schools were established: one for police commanders near

Interesting portrait photo of an officer of the professional wing of the *Landwacht*. He wears a late one-button German M43 'universal field cap', displaying woven versions of the SS eagle above the LW flaming grenade, and silver crown-seam piping. His high-collared ex-Dutch Army tunic bears oversized SS-type collar patches made to fit it, showing the LW grenade in white metal on his right patch and the four 'stars' of a *Stormbanleider* (major) on his left – this being the Dutch translation of the German SS rank of Sturmbannführer. (Beeldbankwo2.nl/ NIOD, & Oorlogs- en Verzetsmuseum Groningen)

Apeldoorn in Gelderland province, and a *politie-opleidingsbataljon* (POB, Police Training Battalion) for the lower ranks at Schalkhaar, a village near Deventer in Overijssel province. The instructors included both SS personnel and fanatical NSB members. In addition to ideological indoctrination and the inculcation of absolute discipline and obedience, and sports activities for improving fitness, the trainees received some military training.

Members of the *Staatspolitie* were referred to as *Schalkhaarders*, 'those from Schalkhaar'; but despite the POB's reputation for Nazi indoctrination it cannot be said that every Schalkhaar-trained officer was a collaborator. For example, it has been documented that some officers left the training programme because they refused to perform the compulsory Hitler salute, and others were dismissed after refusing to take part in a refresher course.

Wachtmannen (Watchmen)

One means of freeing up German manpower for combat service was to hire local Wachmänner (singular, Wachmann; in Dutch, *Wachtmannen*, singular *Wachtman*). These 'Watchmen' guarded all kinds of vulnerable locations: airfields, arsenals and munition stores, factories, bridges and canal locks – but also prisons, and they provided some of the security personnel at the infamous concentration camps at Westerbork and Vught. Initially, Wachmänner were supplied by two German private security companies named Wachdienst Niedersachsen (Guard Service Lower Saxony) and Westdeutscher Wach- und Schutzdienst (West German Guard and Protection

Service). However, they proved to be poorly motivated and ill-disciplined; particularly among those provided by the Wachdienst Niedersachsen, theft and embezzlement were rife.

These problems prompted Gen Christiansen to cancel the contracts with both firms, and on 1 August 1943 he established the Wachabteilung des Chefintendanten beim Wehrmachtbefehlshaber in den Niederlanden ('Guard Unit of the Chief Intendant of the Armed Forces Commander-in-Chief Netherlands'). From then on the reorganized Wachmänner were an integral part of the Wehrmacht, wearing former Dutch Army uniforms dyed a distinctive blueish-green, and carrying weapons (mainly of captured types). Staff training was improved, and discipline became tighter. Because of the good pay and secondary employment benefits, some Dutchmen found the job appealing.

Kontroll-Kommando (KK, Control Guard)

In 1941, Camp Erika was founded near Ommen, a town in the eastern province of Overijssel. In June 1942 it was brought into use as a judicial penal camp to relieve the overcrowded prisons. The prisoners in Erika were guarded by a specially trained unit of Dutchmen known as the Kontroll-Kommando. This KK, which was affiliated to the SS, numbered about 400 men, and its first members were recruited among the unemployed in Amsterdam. The KK guards were infamous for mistreating their prisoners, and later in the war they were also given the task of tracking down people in hiding and Resistance fighters. The KK was dissolved in 1944.

Nederlandse Landwacht (LW, Home Guard)

The year 1943 proved to be a turning-point in the rise of the Dutch Resistance (as discussed below). As an increasing number of NSB members and other Dutch collaborators were assassinated by the Resistance, Dutch Nazis became fearful, and appealed to the German authorities for protection. Consequently, on 12 November 1943, the HSSPF authorized the formation of a militia known as the *Nederlandse Landwacht*. This organization enlisted exclusively NSB party members, and no Germans served in it. The LW consisted of a 'professional' wing of full-time *beroepswachters*, and an 'auxiliary' wing of *hulplandwachters* who served part-time.

Initially, members wore their NSB or WA uniforms, or that of any other collaborationist organization they belonged to. Civilian clothing was to be avoided whenever possible, but nonetheless was often worn by auxiliary LW members who had nothing else. Members of both the full-time and part-time wings wore on the left upper arm a red brassard bearing in two lines 'LANDWACHT/NEDERLAND' in black lettering, flanked by two vertical black *wolfsangels* ('wolf-hook' runic symbols) copied

Cycling group of *Landwacht* part-time auxiliary *hulplandwachters*. They wear assorted civilian clothing, and are identifiable as LW only by their left-arm brassards and the fact that they are openly carrying civilian shotguns – see Plate D2. (Beeldbankwo2.nl/ NIOD)

from the *Germaanse-SS in Nederland*. The auxiliaries were equipped only with shotguns, often of elderly and unreliable models.

In January 1944, SS-Gruf Rauter ordered that henceforth the LW should wear the field-grey uniform of the Waffen-SS, complete with the SS eagle-and-swastika badge on the cap, but photos often show the retention of the NSB/WA's black shirts, riding breeches and boots (see page 22). Their ranks would also be Dutch translations of SS ranks with the associated insignia displayed on the left collar patch. Instead of the SS runes, the right patch would bear a white-metal flaming-grenade badge, clearly borrowed from the *Staatspolitie*. This standardization brought the LW firmly into the realm of the SS, fully under the command of the HSSPF, and reduced the influence of the NSB leadership.

Two original variants of the LW brassard (compare with Plates D1 and D2). The upper example is of cotton with black printed lettering and 'wolf's-hooks', and the lower is of felt with black embroidery. (Anonymous private collection; photo Klaas Castelein)

Initially, the LW was tasked with protecting various administrative offices holding records and permits, and the transport of food-ration coupons (both these being magnets for Resistance raids – see below). Soon other police powers were added, such as checking identity cards, provisionally arresting people perceived to be behaving suspiciously, and confiscating weapons and illegal literature. Rauter was authorized to assign them any other security tasks he felt necessary, and from mid-1944 the LW started mounting security

C COLLABORATION & RESISTANCE

(1) Kontroll-Kommando guard; Camp Erika, 1942–44
Only a few photos of the KK are known, but based on these and a detailed description of the uniform this reconstruction is possible; to the best of our knowledge, it is the first to be published. The KK wore the slightly blueish 'field grey' uniform of the former Dutch Army, but trimmed with SS buttons, a Dutch-made SS collar patch bearing 'K.K.' in white, and a black cuff title edged and lettered 'K.K.' in white. On the Dutch Army sidecap they displayed the SS death's-head badge, but no eagle. Minimal rifle equipment was issued: the Waffen-SS enlisted ranks' belt, with either two or three Dutch black leather M95 ammunition pouches attached each side of the buckle. The weapon was the 6.5mm Dutch M95 Hembrug (Mannlicher) rifle.

(2) Wachmann, after August 1943
After the Watchmen were absorbed into the Wehrmacht in August 1943 they were issued former Dutch Army uniforms dyed a blueish-green shade, which earned them the mocking civilian nicknames of *groene kikkers* ('green frogs') or *petroleummannetjes* ('little petrol men'). The cap is the standard German M43 Einheitsfeldmütze ('universal field cap'), also dyed blue-green, and bearing machine-woven German Army insignia on a truncated triangular backing. He displays German Army M40 collar patches with infantry-white 'lights', and the standard eagle-and-swastika badge above his right breast pocket, but because he has no rank his shoulder

straps are plain. Dutch puttees and M37 Dutch Army ankle boots complete the uniform, with a German Army enlisted ranks' belt. The Watchmen were armed with assorted rifles, predominantly of Italian or captured Dutch and French models; this trainee is loading a 7.5mm French MAS36 (German designation Gewehr 242f). As far as is known, this is the first visual reconstruction of the Wachmann uniform.

(3) *Landelijke Knokploegen* fighter, after August 1943
The most obvious feature of this reconstruction of a KP fighter, taking part in a raid to capture documents from a town hall, is that his elderly ex-police or Army revolver has no cylinder, and is thus useless for anything more than bluffing the most ignorant of civil servants. In 1942–44, after the halt in Allied arms drops due to the Abwehr's success in intercepting them, the LKP and RVV faced a dire shortage of weapons. (For instance, before the resumption of supplies from September 1944, the entire KP in Friesland province had no more than 50 firearms; and no more than 40 per cent of the entire KP in Limburg province were armed even with pistols.)

This volunteer wears civilian clothes including a leather coat and a 'Breton' sailor-style cap. It is recorded that some KP members wore 'Zorro'-type masks to conceal their identity from local fellow-countrymen. The National Prison Museum in Veenhuizen, a village in Drenthe province, displays such a mask which was worn by a KP member who participated in the famously successful prison raid in Leeuwarden in early December 1944.

Various patterns of original LW cuff titles, showing different fonts and differences in manufacture.
(Top) Officer's type, hand-embroidered in aluminium thread.
(Second & fifth) Supplied blank and printed in the Netherlands.
(Third & fourth) White cotton machine embroidery.
(Anonymous private collection; photo Klaas Castelein)

Group of full-time LW *beroepswachters* photographed in Haren, a town in Groningen province. Those dressed in black are wearing the uniform of the NSB's paramilitary WA, with added LW brassards. The others are dressed in what might be regarded as a compromise between the HSSPF's orders, and the wishes of the NSB *Leider* Anton Mussert: they wear Waffen-SS caps and tunics, complete with cuff titles, but retain the NSB/WA's black breeches – compare with Plate D1. (Beeldbankwo2. nl/ NIOD)

patrols, which made them one of the most hated paramilitary formations in the occupied Netherlands. While arbitrarily detaining civilians to check their identity documents, they often 'confiscated' any items of value.

After September 1944, many LW members fled from the advancing Allied forces into the still-occupied northern provinces. There they cooperated with the Sipo in arresting people in hiding, hunting down Resistance members, mistreating prisoners, and terrorizing the local population. In the very last phase of the war the LW was organized into nominal battalions and companies, and the auxiliaries' shotguns were replaced with army rifles, usually of older Italian or Dutch types. In April 1945, LW units under the authority of local Wehrmacht commanders took part in fighting against the rapidly advancing Canadians and British.

Landstorm Nederland
(LSN, Territorial Defence Force)

Prior to the establishment of the *Nederlandse Landwacht* in November 1943, on 12 March 1943 a military territorial defence force had been created, initially called the *Landwacht Nederland*. (Needless to say, these virtually identical titles have created confusion ever since.) Shortly before the creation of the LW, on 16 October 1943 the existing territorial defence force was renamed as the *Landstorm Nederland* (LSN), operating under the control of the SS.

There was initially considerable interest in joining the LSN. In the prevailing conditions of scarcity and unemployment, many Dutchmen enlisted for the sake of wages and regular meals, and to avoid forced labour. Since the LSN confined its operations to Dutch territory, there was no anxiety about being transferred to the Russian Front. In October 1943 the LSN numbered some 2,400 men, and by mid-1944 it was about 3,400 strong. As mentioned above, it included an NJS youth company (which was briefly deployed, reportedly in the ranks of Kampfgruppe von Tettau, against the British 1st Abn Div during the battle of Arnhem in September 1944).

A young Dutch Waffen-SS soldier of the *Landstorm Nederland* regiment; probably serving with the 3rd *(Jeugdstorm)* Company of the LSN's III Battalion, he was photographed in the Utrechtseweg in Arnhem just after the fighting of 17-25 September 1944. Most members of the LSN wore these plain black right collar patches, though others displayed the LW's flaming grenade, and some Waffen-SS veterans the SS-runes to which they were entitled. The missing right shoulder strap is not thought to be significant. (Gelders Archief)

On 1 November 1944, the three-battalion regiment was redesignated as SS-Freiwilligen Grenadier Brigade 'Landstorm Nederland'; this reportedly had a strength of 7,000–8,000, after significant numbers were drafted in from the *Germaanse-SS in Nederland* (see MAA 420, *The Waffen-SS (4): 24. to 38. Divisions & Volunteer Legions*). Although weakened by desertions as the prospect of fighting the Allied armies became a reality, in February 1945 the formation was retitled 'on paper' as 34. SS-Frw Gren Div 'Landstorm Nederland'. This divisional status was purely nominal; by then it barely had the strength of a brigade, structured as SS-Frw Gren Regts 83 and 84, an anti-tank Panzerjäger Abteilung and a Flak Bataillon, of uncertain size and levels of equipment.

Following the battle of Arnhem, in the last seven months of the war the LSN engaged in the fight against the 'internal enemies' of the Resistance movement, and in the process many innocent civilians would also fall victim to its methods. The SS-Wachbataillon 'Nordwest' of Regt 84, commanded by SS-Standartenführer (colonel, SS-Staf) Michael Lippert, became particularly notorious, for instance for shooting out of hand Dutch civilians who ventured into a Sperrgebiet ('prohibited area'). Various members of the LSN were assigned to other quasi-military duties, including guarding Camp Erika near Ommen.

The LSN clung to its weapons as long as possible. Since its members had good reason to fear the vengeance of their countrymen, they were naturally anxious to surrender to Allied troops and not to the Dutch Resistance. Even after the German surrender at Wageningen on 5 May 1945, parts of the LSN

A poor-quality but historic photograph, showing the eventual surrender to the British 49th Inf Div, on 9 May 1945, of the LSN remnant that had been holding out in Veenendaal. Over the previous days they had subjected the townspeople to a reign of terror. For instance, on 7 May, the battalion sergeant-major, SS-Hauptscharführer Evert Verton – seen here front centre, wearing a 'crusher cap' – had shot and paralyzed for life a 14-year-old boy. (Veenendaal Municipality)

refused to capitulate. This was the case in Veenendaal, a municipality in the central province of Utrecht, which survived the Wehrmacht's surrender as an enclave of Germans and Dutch collaborators. On 1 May, *Groep Albrecht*, a Resistance group specializing in gathering military intelligence, had reported the strength of this isolated force at about 1,300, of whom some 900 were SS-men.

Frightened by the Axis defeat, and drunk on gin, the Dutch SS in Veenendaal terrorized the local population. On 6 May 1945, the Vaart Bridge in Veenendaal was blown up, unintentionally killing two Dutch SS-men. On the same day a clash took place between SS soldiers from Veenendaal and a reconnaissance group of 12 resistance fighters from nearby Wageningen, in which three of the latter were killed. Eventually, the LSN element in Veenendaal surrendered to the British 49th (West Riding) Inf Div only on 9 May 1945.

GROWTH OF THE RESISTANCE, 1940–44

Continuing the fight from Great Britain

On 13 May 1940, when the German invasion campaign was reaching its climax in the Netherlands, Queen Wilhelmina and her government were evacuated to England by the British destroyers HMS *Hereward* and *Windsor* (see also MAA 493, *Hitler's Blitzkrieg Enemies 1940*). Leading her London-based government-in-exile, Queen Wilhelmina became to many Dutch the symbolic figurehead of the Resistance. Approximately 1,700 men and women also succeeded by various means in reaching Great Britain, from where they would continue the fight against Nazi Germany. These people were popularly referred to as *Engelandvaarders*, meaning 'those sailing to England'. Those who managed to reach Britain were personally received by the queen, who sought any news about the situation in her occupied country.

While the struggle of Dutch exiles lies outside the scope of this book, their service should be acknowledged (see MAA 238, *Foreign Volunteers of the Allied Forces 1939-45*). Many of these men and women would serve as Special Operations Executive (SOE) agents; as soldiers in the *Princes Irene* Brigade, or in No. 2 (Dutch) Troop of No. 10 (Inter-Allied) Commando; on board British or Dutch warships and merchant vessels; or as flying personnel with the Dutch Nos. 320, 321 and 322 Sqns of the British RAF.

(The most famous of these exiles was probably the so-called '*Soldaat van Oranje*' Erik Hazelhoff Roelfzema, a young prewar writer and a student activist in 1940-41. Reaching Britain as a stowaway in summer 1941, he subsequently served as an SOE agent, making many dangerous sea crossings to deliver radios and pick up resistance fighters in small boats. Hazelhoff Roelfzema qualified as a pilot in 1942, going on to fly 72 combat missions in DH Mosquito bombers with No.139 Sqn of the RAF's elite Pathfinder Force. When Queen Wilhelmina returned to her country on 13 March 1945, this highly-decorated officer acted as her adjutant.)

When considering the growth and organization of the Resistance on Dutch soil, it should be borne in mind that the movement was by no means a monolithic entity. Resistance was manifested in many forms and layers of activity; sometimes these were interwoven, sometimes they operated independently. While using the generic term 'Dutch Resistance', we concentrate here on the most relevant examples of armed underground groups, but readers should understand that this short account cannot claim to be exhaustive.

Jan Verleun, photographed in Dutch Army uniform; during the May 1940 campaign he was wounded while serving at Fort Westervoort, on the IJssel river in Gelderland province. Following the surrender he joined the Amsterdam-based *CS-6* resistance group, and was co-responsible for the assassination of LtGen Seyffardt, honorary commander of the SS-Freiwilligen Legion 'Nederland', on 5 February 1943. Verleun evaded the immediate German reaction, but was arrested on 4 November 1943, and executed on 7 January 1944. (Conserve Uitgeverij)

The 'England Game'

No such account can avoid mention of the Germans' so-called Englandspiel ('England Game'), which was pursued by the Abwehr military intelligence branch and the SD against the British SOE.

In early 1942 this German effort (officially codenamed Nordpol, 'Operation *North Pole*') secured access to the radio codes used between the SOE and the Dutch underground Order Service (see below). As a result, between March 1942 and May 1943, dozens of Dutch SOE secret agents sent from Great Britain to the Netherlands fell into German hands. Tragically, the Germans successfully deceived the SOE into believing that these agents were still at large and operational, and consequently the British continued to send agents and supplies to the Netherlands. In total, about 200 Dutch nationals were arrested as a result, of whom some 130 died at the hands of the German security services or in concentration camps. The disastrous effects of the Englandspiel did not remain confined to the Dutch Resistance; Belgian and French underground organizations were also infiltrated as a result, and in total the Germans claimed that 'Nordpol' led to the arrest of more than 400 Dutch, Belgian and French resistance members.

Truus Oversteegen (left) and Hannie Schaft (right) were both members of the RVV's Haarlem group, and were among the few women Resistance members who engaged in assassinating Germans and Dutch collaborators. In this photo, taken before or after such a mission, Oversteegen is carrying a weapon (probably a semi-automatic FN pistol) in her bag, and is dressed as a man, to make the couple less immediately conspicuous. Schaft had dyed her hair black and adopted a pair of glasses to disguise herself. (Beeldbankwo2.nl/ NIOD & Verzetsmuseum Amsterdam)

Apart from the loss of human lives (often in the cruellest circumstances), large quantities of weapons, explosives, radio equipment and other supplies destined for the Dutch Resistance fell into German hands. In total, the Germans intercepted about 15,000kg (14.75 tons) of explosives, 800 Sten sub-machine guns, 60 Bren light machine guns, 2,300 handguns, 50,000 rounds of ammunition, 8,000 hand grenades, 75 radio transmitters, and 450,000 Dutch guilders in cash. When the British finally became aware of the true situation, airdrops destined for the Resistance were suspended, and only resumed from September 1944 onwards. Consequently, during the mid-war years the Dutch Resistance suffered from a dire shortage of weapons.

There was another indirect consequence during the battle of Arnhem in September 1944, when, notoriously, the British 1st Abn Div's radio communications failed. Probably as a hangover from the Englandspiel debacle, officers were unwilling to use the functioning telephone network offered them by the local Dutch Resistance.

EMERGENCE OF THE FIRST RESISTANCE MOVEMENTS

Communistische Partij Nederland
(CPN, Netherlands Communist Party)

One of the first resistance movements to emerge was the Netherlands Communist Party. As early as 15 May 1940, the day after the Dutch Army's surrender, the CPN held a meeting to plan its underground survival and operations against the Nazi authorities.

It was the CPN which called the country's first general strike, in response to Orpo raids in Amsterdam on 22 February 1941 which arrested 427 Jews for deportation. At about noon on 25 February strikes brought Amsterdam to a halt, and many other cities followed suit. SS-Gruppenführer Rauter declared martial law, and the German authorities quelled the strike with heavy-handed tactics, opening fire almost immediately and arresting many strikers. This was the only occasion during World War II that a population in German-occupied territory openly protested against the Nazi persecution of Jews. Between summer 1941 and summer 1942 the CPN went on to make an important contribution to the various forms of resistance, including the assassination of perceived collaborators.

Following the first round-up in Amsterdam, the application of anti-Jewish laws steadily increased. Regular trainloads of Jewish deportees began to leave for the East in July 1942, carrying what would finally total some 110,000 men, women and children to the extermination camps – mainly to Auschwitz and Sobibor. Of these, only about 8,000 would survive the war. Bounties were offered by the German authorities for the betrayal of Jewish fugitives, and were claimed by some collaborators (though it should be noted that other Dutch civilians would later be honoured by the state of Israel for sheltering Jews).

Geuzen ('Beggars')

On the same day that the CPN held its first meeting to organize underground resistance, a Haarlem-born teacher named Bernardus IJzerdraat wrote his first leaflet protesting against the German occupation, and calling upon the public to resist. The distribution of IJzerdraat's leaflets were the first acts of public resistance, and he is generally regarded as a pioneer of resistance warfare in the Netherlands. He started to build a resistance organization called the *Geuzen* (a corruption of the French word *gueux*, 'beggars', and thus echoing a Spanish insult proudly adopted by late 16th-century Dutch insurgents).

IJzerdraat intended to establish a clandestine network of agents to carry out, among other tasks, espionage and sabotage. He travelled throughout the country, appointing people he deemed to be reliable to set up resistance cells. While seeking to mobilize his fellow countrymen IJzerdraat claimed that he had already established contact with Great Britain; this was not the case, but it increased the appeal of his cause, and several *Geuzen* groups were founded in and around Rotterdam. As with other early resistance groups, they made naive mistakes, since the Dutch people had no experience whatever of resistance warfare. Some members were careless in discussing their emerging organization, oblivious to the fact that the German security services were experienced in tracking down political opponents and suppressing dissent.

The *Geuzen* only succeeded in carrying out a few acts of sabotage. In the Rotterdam area the electricity cable of a searchlight battery was cut, as were German telephone lines in the nearby Hook of Holland. In some cases German soldiers, either sentries or strolling around off-duty, were killed and their bodies secretly disposed of. As a result of too much careless talk, the *Geuzen* groups were quickly rounded up throughout the western province of South Holland, and hundreds of members ended up in the

The Oversteegen sisters Truus (left) and Freddie (right), posing with two male NBS fighters shortly after the May 1945 Liberation. Only 15 when the war began, during the Occupation Freddie braided her hair in two plaits so as to look even younger and less suspicious. Given their Communist background, the sisters felt uncomfortable when, in September 1944, the RVV was absorbed into the Netherlands Interior Forces, since this unified underground army was dominated by more right-wing elements. (National Hannie Schaft Foundation)

infamous *'Oranjehotel'* prison in the Scheveningen suburb of The Hague.[3]

On 25 November 1940, Bernard IJzerdraat himself was arrested in Haarlem. On 13 March 1941 he, 14 other *Geuzen*, and three of the February 1941 strikers were executed. This was the first mass execution in the Netherlands, and it made a great impression both within and beyond the fledgling Resistance.

One of the regular tasks of the Resistance was trying to rescue shot-down Allied aircrew before they could be captured by the Germans. An American airman named H.S. Mann, here supported by bystanders, was the only crew member to bale out successfully from a bomber shot down near Zwolle in Overijssel province on 11 January 1944. Although Mann was captured shortly after this photo was taken, numbers of other US and British airmen did manage to contact the Resistance, and were hidden until they could be passed on to safety. (Historisch Centrum Overijssel)

Ordedienst (OD, Order Service)

One of the first major armed resistance movements to be created was the Order Service, organized during the summer of 1940. In popular perception, the OD consisted solely of ex-Dutch Army officers and was organized along military lines. It was thus seen purely as the underground continuation of the pre-war Army, known for having a right-wing and conservative orientation. The reality, however, turned out to be more complex. The OD certainly had a considerable number of ex-Army men among its members, but civilians also joined. For instance, on 6 February 1943, when the German authorities put 100 imprisoned OD members on 'death row' for anticipated reprisal shootings, 58 of these so-called Todeskandidaten ('death candidates') lacked any military background at all.

Initially, the OD's main self-appointed role was preparing to maintain public order during an eventual transition from occupation to liberation. However, as the German occupation dragged on, the OD also engaged in collecting and transmitting intelligence to London (see above, 'The England Game'), in sabotaging telephone lines and railways, and in circulating descriptions of collaborators. At one point the OD boasted that it could muster an army of 100,000, but it has been estimated that active members in fact numbered no more than about 4,000. To the disappointment of many in the OD, in the event their organization was not empowered to act as an interim authority during the liberation of the Netherlands in 1944–45; that role was entrusted to the *Militaire Gezag* (MG, Military Authority), established by the Dutch government-in-exile from London.

CS-6

Like the OD, the Amsterdam-based resistance group *CS-6* was established in the summer of 1940, but since few of its members would survive the war the record of its history is still incomplete. It is generally believed that the initials referred to the street address where the group was created: Corellistraat 6 in Amsterdam. *CS-6* was known for its youthful membership and left-wing orientation, numbering among its members Communist students, artists

---

3 The total of roughly 25,000 prisoners detained in this facility during the war also included Jews, Jehovah's Witnesses, black-market traders, etc, but it was already nicknamed 'Hotel Orange' in honour of the Resistance prisoners. 'Orange', after the name of the Dutch royal house, was a common shorthand term for the Resistance.

and other educated young people, mostly in their twenties. The group was engaged in collecting weapons, committing sabotage, and assassinating collaborators. It was led by Dr Gerrit Kastein, a CPN member; born in 1910, he was older than most of his comrades, and during the Spanish Civil War (1936–39) he had served as a medical volunteer with the Republican forces.

The most prominent victim of a CS-6 assassination was LtGen Hendrik Seyffardt, a staunchly anti-Communist and pro-German retired Dutch senior commander.[4] Seyffardt was the honorary (but not field) commander of the Waffen-SS Volunteer Legion 'Nederland', and also a member of Anton Mussert's 'shadow cabinet'. Late on 5 February 1943 two CS-6 members rang his doorbell; when he opened the door he was shot, but he did not succumb to his wounds before describing his killers as apparently students. Some ascribe the assassination of Seyffardt to Gerrit Kastein and Jan Verleun, a veteran of the May 1940 campaign; others believe that Verleun carried it out with Leo Frijda, a Jewish resistance fighter. Starting on 6 February, SS-Gruf Rauter's reprisals saw a number of hostages shot, and the arrest of some 600 students at universities and colleges in Amsterdam, Delft, Utrecht and Wageningen. Gerrit Kastein was arrested on 19 February. Shortly after being detained he threw himself out of an upper window, presumably to prevent himself from giving information under torture; he survived the fall, but died a few hours later.

Another renowned CS-6 member was the woman author Reina Prinsen Geerligs. She was involved in hiding and caring for fugitives, escorting Jewish children from one hiding-place to another, falsifying documents, distributing illegal literature, transporting weapons, and acting as a

In early February 1944, an Assault Team (*knokploeg*, KP) of the LO organization successfully raided the town hall of Burgum (formerly Bergum) in the northern province of Friesland. In this wartime artist's impression, note the raiders wearing 'Zorro' masks (see also Plate C3), and the getaway car visible through the window. On this occasion the proceeds amounted to 18,000 *controlezegels* (security labels to be applied to identity documents), 584 blank identity cards, and about 500 guilders in cash. (Beeldbankwo2.nl/ NIOD & Fries Verzetsmuseum)

4   For more details on Gen Seyffardt, see also MAA 531, *Dutch Waffen-SS Legion and Brigade, 1941–44*.

lookout when an assassination was carried out. On 23 July 1943 she was arrested while delivering a pistol to a CS-6 venue. She and another arrested member confessed to the Germans to having assassinated Pieter Kaay, a collaborationist police officer; there is reason to believe that this confession was false, and made simply in order to protect those actually responsible. On 23 November 1943, the 21-year-old Prinsen Geerligs and two other female members were executed in Sachsenhausen concentration camp; according to witnesses, the three women met their deaths singing, and with their heads held high.

Eventually, the Germans succeeded in rounding up the remainder of CS-6, executing 33 of its members (including both Frijda and Verleun, who were executed on 1 October 1943 and 7 January 1944 respectively).

Raad van Verzet (RVV, Resistance Council)

On 20 April 1943, this Council of Resistance was founded by eight men, of whom one was Jan Thijssen, a former OD radio operator known as *Lange Jan* ('Long John'). Thijssen found the OD too passive, and wanted to engage in more active and aggressive forms of resistance. Consequently, he and seven like-minded comrades established the RVV (also referred to simply as the *Raad*, 'Council'). The RVV hoped to become an umbrella organization that would coordinate all kinds of resistance activities across

---

D COUNTER-RESISTANCE

(1) Professional Rottenführer, *Landwacht*, after January 1944
This corporal of the full-time LW *beroepswachters* wears a black-painted German M42 helmet, with a white-on-black *'wolfsangel'* rune decal. This symbol, and his black shirt, tie, breeches and riding boots, all identify his parent organization, the Dutch National Socialist Movement's WA paramilitary wing. Alternatively, the professional wing of the LW might wear black Dutch M34 helmets, displaying either this WA 'wolf-hook' or the LW's flaming-grenade badge – as visible here on the crown of the field-grey M43 'universal field cap' tucked into his Waffen-SS enlisted ranks' belt. His field-grey Waffen-SS M40 tunic is worn with the collar opened; the right-hand collar patch bears the LW flaming grenade in white metal (see also **1a**), while the left patch shows the two narrow silver braids of his rank of Rottenführer. On his left upper arm he wears a red brassard, lettered in black 'LANDWACHT/ NEDERLAND' between two *wolfsangels*, and around his forearm one of several variants of the SS-style 'LANDWACHT' cuff title. Wearing the brassard was compulsory for both uniformed (professional) and ununiformed (auxiliary) LW men, but in most photographs of professional members the cuff title alone is worn. This NCO is armed with a 9mm Walther P38, carried butt-forwards in a 'hard-shell' leather holster.

(1a) LW collar patch
Professional LW members wore this white-metal *vlammende granaat*, clearly inherited from the *Staatspolitie*, on their right collar patch. This was also worn by some *Landstorm Nederland* personnel.

(2) Auxiliary LW member, after November 1943
This rough rural type can only be identified as a *hulplandwachter* part-time LW auxiliary by his red brassard, and by the fact that he is openly carrying a weapon – typically, an external-hammer 16-bore shotgun. These led to a mocking

nickname for the unpopular auxiliaries – *Jan Hagel* ('John Hail', in reference to the shotguns' 'hailshot' pellets).

(3) Flemish Untersturmführer, Sicherheitsdienst; Friesland, April 1945
This figure is partly based on a photograph of a notorious Flemish SD officer named Emil Steylaerts, who was based at Crackstate, a prison at Heerenveen in Friesland province. Driven from his Belgian homeland by the Allied advance in 1944, he was one of those SD men who continued to fight against the Resistance, in mixed-nationality units based in the Dutch northern provinces, until the final arrival of Canadian troops.

Generally, the SD wore the same uniforms as the Waffen-SS with minor insignia variations. His unstiffened 'old-style officer's field cap' (to modern collectors, a 'crusher cap') bears the usual woven SS eagle and death's-head badges. The crown- and band-piping was officially in 'poison-green' Waffenfarbe for the SD, but standard infantry-white was also common. Unusually, he wears over his uniform an unbadged Luftwaffe M42 'splinter-pattern' camouflage jacket instead of a Waffen-SS smock. The exposed collar of his M43 field-grey tunic bears black SS patches with officers' aluminium-cord edging; his left patch shows the three 'stars' of second-lieutenant's rank, but in the SD the right patch was plain. The field-grey M43 Rundbundhose or Keilhose ('round-' or 'wedge-trousers ') are tucked into early-war Wehrmacht marching boots. He is armed with a 9mm MP40 sub-machine gun, with spare magazines in the pair of canvas triple pouches worn on an SS enlisted-ranks' belt. An M24 stick grenade is thrust ready to hand into one of his boots. The display of awards (the Infantry Assault Badge, and silver Wound Badge) on his left chest confirm previous battle experience; before he transferred to the SD he had probably served with the Flemish 6. SS-Sturmbrigade 'Langemarck' on the Eastern Front (see MAA 539, *Belgian Waffen-SS Legions and Brigades 1941–44*).

LEGITIMATIE №. 3425

LANDELIJKE ORGANISATIE VOOR HULP AAN ONDERDUIKERS (L.O.)

Leden van erkende verzetsorganisaties, militaire en burgerlijke autoriteiten worden dringend verzocht bezitter dezer papieren alle mogelijke hulp en inlichtingen te geven.

Ondergeteekende is _____ van de L.O.

Kenmerken van het persoonsbewijs: Naam: *Brouwer*

Voornamen: *Hielke Willem*

Geboren te: *Achtung Achtkarspelen*

Geboortedatum: *19 Juli 1890*

Beroep: *Onderwijzer*

No. *A11/001411*

Namens het C.B.: de Districtsleider: de Houder:

NED. BINNENLANDSCHE STRIJDKRACHTEN
Interior military forces of the Netherlands

Bij dezen wordt verklaard dat
This is to certify that

Naam
Surname *Brouwer*

Voornaam
Christian name *Hielke*

Persoonsbewijs
Identity-card No. *A11-001411*

Area
Adres *Trynwâlden 161*

Behoort tot
Belongs to *N.B.S.*
Friesland

Onderdeel
Army-unit *1.4. Gem. S.K.*

Functie- Rang
Function- Grade *I.II. Gem SK*

De Gewestelijke Cdt. v. d. Ordedienst (O.D.)
The Regional Commander „Ordedienst" (O.D.)

Op last
By order

Datum van afgifte
Date of issue *10. 4. 45*

1944

GEW. FRIESLAND
Stempel
Seal
NBS

Hielke Brouwer headed the LO organization in Achtkarspelen, a municipality in Friesland, where his main task was allocating shelter for Jewish fugitives. Like many LD-LKP members, his willingness to resist was largely informed by his Protestant beliefs. However, during the final stage of the war he also joined the Netherlands Interior Forces. (Left) is his LO identity card, and (right) his NBS card, thus neatly illustrating the blurred boundary between non-violent and armed resistance. The NBS card is signed by Capt Arie Meijer, overall commander of the NBS in Friesland; interestingly, immediately above his signature the OD (Order Service) initials have been replaced with those of the NBS. (Courtesy Ieke Jan Sevinga; photo Klaas Castelein, digitally edited by Sjoerd van der Zande)

the country. Although it never achieved this goal, it certainly became one of the most influential armed resistance groups in the Netherlands.

It was perceived by many, including the predominantly conservative OD, as a Communist or leftist-revolutionary organization, but this perception was far from the reality on the ground. The RVV's following in the western province of North Holland certainly included a considerable number of Communists, but other political and religious tendencies were also represented. For instance, the RVV group in Haarlem, the provincial capital of North Holland, consisted of Communists, Trotskyists, anarchists, Christians, Freemasons, and non-aligned volunteers. Most members of the RVV in Rotterdam, the major port in South Holland province, had liberal leanings, and their leaders sought to keep Communists out of their 1,000-strong 'brigade' (of whom some 500 could be armed, and about 150 took part in active operations). The RVV in the Veluwe, a wooded region in the eastern province of Gelderland, consisted of both non-religious volunteers and practising Protestants. In short, the RVV as a whole had no strongly expressed political or religious orientation, and embraced a wide range of affiliations.

One ambush staged by the RVV, near the village of Putten in the Veluwe, triggered particularly disastrous repercussions. On the night of 30 September/1 October 1944, RVV fighters ambushed a military vehicle carrying four German soldiers. The team's Bren-gunner was actually the British Sgt Keith Banwell of 10th Bn, Parachute Regt, who had escaped capture after Operation *Market Garden* and linked up with the Resistance. In the chaotic fight that ensued, the German Lt Sommer and one RVV fighter were killed. In reprisals (ordered by Gen Christiansen, not by SS-Ogruf Rauter), the Germans cordoned off Putten, burnt down more than 100 houses, and deported more than 600 male inhabitants aged 18 to 50. The great majority of these were sent via Camp Amersfoort to Neuengamme concentration camp, which few would survive. In total, 552 civilians died as a result of this German reprisal.[5]

Three women RVV fighters

While women played many and vital roles throughout the Resistance as a whole, only a limited number of them engaged in actual assassinations. The RVV group in Haarlem, which was commanded by Frans van der Wiel, attracted considerable attention during and after the war, not least because it included three women who did carry out a number of such missions: the Oversteegen sisters Truus (born 1923) and Freddie (b. 1925), and Hannie Schaft (b. 1920).

Raised by an idealistic Communist mother, the Oversteegen sisters became involved during the 1930s in providing clandestine refuge in their home for fugitives from Nazi Germany. In those years persecuted Jews, Communists and socialists were smuggled from Germany to the Netherlands by organizations such as *Rode Hulp* ('Red Aid'); this was forbidden by the Dutch government, which was anxious not to risk compromising its neutrality. When the war reached the Netherlands the sisters continued their anti-fascist struggle within the framework of the Resistance, including the killing of off-duty German soldiers and Dutch collaborators.

Hannie Schaft, a Communist-inspired law student who was appalled by the persecution of Jewish citizens, also linked up with the Haarlem branch of the RVV. From her conspicuous chestnut-brown hair Schaft became famous as *het meisje met het rode haar* ('the red-haired girl'). Once her physical appearance became known to the Germans, she dyed her hair black and adopted glasses in order to disguise herself. The Oversteegen sisters and Schaft teamed up for a number of operations.

On 21 March 1945, Schaft was intercepted at a checkpoint, where the security personnel found the illegal Communist resistance newspaper *De Waarheid* ('The Truth') in her bicycle bag, and after her arrest a 9mm FN pistol in her handbag. Her identity was finally confirmed during her subsequent imprisonment and interrogation, when the red roots of her hair began to grow through. On 17 April 1945, less than a month before the Liberation, Hannie Schaft was executed in the Overveen sand dunes near Bloemendaal on the coast west of Haarlem. Legend has it that the first volley only wounded her slightly, prompting her to remark defiantly '*Ik schiet beter!*' ('I can shoot better than that!'), and this provoked the infamous

On 11 June 1944 an Assault Team led by LKP leader Liepke Scheepstra (alias 'Bob') raided a prison in Arnhem, Gelderland, freeing 54 prisoners without firing a shot – one of the greatest successes of the Resistance. This photo of an apparently peaceful street scene was taken immediately afterwards by Scheepstra himself. The man with the bicycle is Johannes ter Horst, one of the raiders, who had approached the prison director disguised as a Protestant clergyman. The woman and little girl are two of the freed prisoners, believed to be Jewish. A month beforehand, on 11 May, the same KP had successfully raided another prison in Arnhem and freed two prisoners, including the LO co-founder Rev Frits Slomp. (Beeldbankwo2.nl/ NIOD)

5 In September 1944, Reichskommissar Seys-Inquardt had authorized both Christiansen and Rauter to inflict 'summary justice' on their own judgement. Condemned to death for war crimes during the Nuremberg trials, Seyss-Inquart was hanged in October 1946. In 1948 a Dutch court sentenced Christiansen to 12 years' imprisonment, but in the event he was released in December 1951.

Before joining the Parachute Regt, 'Tex' Banwell had already served with both the LRDG and the Commandos, and had been captured and had escaped twice, once in North Africa and once in Crete. Captured again following this action, he would survive interrogation by the Gestapo and four months in Auschwitz. For details, see on-line at pegasusarchive.org/arnhem/tex_banwell.htm

Jacques Crasborn (left, showing off a captured Organization Todt officer's cap and tunic) was the KP leader in Limburg province. As such, he stayed in touch with the joint KP force which operated for 66 days in the woods of Baarlo; during this hazardous operation in September – November 1944, he visited them on more than one occasion. Once northern Limburg was liberated, Crasborn joined the ST Shock Forces. (NIMH)

Dutch SD agent Maarten Kuiper to empty his machine-pistol into her. (After the war, Kuiper would be convicted and executed for war crimes.) The Oversteegen sisters both survived the war, but for them the Liberation was overshadowed by the loss of their dear comrade.

Landelijke Organisatie voor Hulp aan Onderduikers (LO, National Organization for Help to People in Hiding)

A form of non-violent resistance that cannot be ignored is the widespread aid to those in hiding. Various categories of people sought to escape the Nazi authorities: German Jews and Communists who had fled to the Netherlands before May 1940, and thereafter thousands of Dutch Jews; Belgian and French escapers from PoW camps in Germany; shot-down Allied airmen; Dutch former PoWs who refused to report for registration, and other men seeking to evade forced labour; students who refused to sign a pledge of loyalty; and civil servants and police officers who refused various orders imposed by the German authorities. The total number of people in hiding in the latter part of the war has been estimated at more than 300,000.

It became obvious that only a nation-wide organization could meet the needs of so many 'submerged' people, and, in February 1943, the National Organization for Help to People in Hiding (simply 'LO' for short) was established. Two figures who were particularly instrumental in this were a *dominee* (Protestant clergyman), the Rev Frits Slomp, and a Protestant housewife and mother of five, Mrs Heleen Kuipers-Rietberg. Travelling from place to place to drum up support, Slomp became known as *Frits de Zwerver*, 'Fritz the Wanderer', while Mrs Kuipers-Rietberg used the pseudonym *Tante Riek* ('Auntie Riek'). In about May 1944 she was betrayed and had to go into hiding herself, but in vain: eventually, she died of disease in Ravensbrück concentration camp in late December 1944. Although arrested by the NSB, the Rev Slomp was rescued, and survived the war.

Many women naturally played significant roles in the LO, which initially expanded through the structures of the Protestant Church, but later became more religiously diverse as it spread across the country into the predominantly Catholic southern provinces.

THE DECISIVE GENERAL STRIKE, APRIL–MAY 1943

Regarded as a turning-point in the history of the Dutch Resistance, this was triggered by the order on 29 April 1943 for Dutch ex-PoWs to report to the authorities for registration. The strike broke out that day in Hengelo, a municipality in the eastern province of Overijssel, and quickly spread throughout the rest of the Netherlands. It had various local names, including *Melkstaking* ('Milk Strike'), because farmers refused to deliver milk to the dairies, and either gave it out for free or poured it away. In the mining region in the southern province of Limburg it came to be known as the *Mijnstaking* ('Mine Strike'), and was supported by the locally-active Roman Catholic Church. With about 200,000 participants, the April–May strike was the largest in the wartime Netherlands. The German authorities employed ruthless methods to suppress it; SS-Gruf Rauter declared a 'special police state of siege', and had about 200 people executed. This episode was a catalyst for the subsequent growth of various resistance organizations, both armed and non-violent.

Landelijke Knokploegen (LKP, National Assault Teams)

Becoming responsible for an ever-growing population of people in hiding, the LO needed an armed wing to back up its more peaceful clandestine activities. Thus, in August 1943, the National Assault Teams (LKP) came into being.

It should be noted that there was no clear distinction between the LO and the LKP. In many cases, an individual resistance member might carry out both 'LO work', non-violent in nature, and 'LKP duties', which involved armed missions. Many would simply speak of the 'LO-LKP' as if it were a single entity; LKP members often regarded the LO as the *Moederorganisatie* or 'mother organization', reminding us that the LKP grew out of the LO.

In addition, it sometimes also occurred that RVV and LKP members would team up for missions, thus further blurring the boundary between these armed organizations.

This photo of resistance fighters posing in North Brabant province is dated 19 September 1944, and bears on the reverse the initials 'K.P.', suggesting that they were still operating as an independent Assault Team although the unified Netherlands Interior Forces had already been formally announced. Under magnification, the letters 'Brab(ant)' can be made out on the brassard worn by the man second from right; the left-hand man's brassard reads 'ORANJE'. (Private photo, unknown wartime source; Klaas Castelein Collection)

A priority for the LKP was raiding town halls, administrative offices and distribution centres to obtain food-ration coupons and blank identity documents; these vital papers were badly needed by the LO, since 'submerged' people had no legal access to them. The LKP were also tasked with destroying civil registry records that contained incriminating information (for instance, mentioning someone's Jewish background), with freeing political prisoners, and with liquidating Germans and Dutch collaborators.

A single assault team was known as a *knokploeg* (KP). In late August 1944 there were about 45 of these nation-wide, totalling some 750 active fighters. These teams differed in size, socio-economic composition, and religious or political affiliation; the one thing they all had in common was their shortage of weapons. Some so-called 'wild KPs' did not operate within the overall LKP command structure, and fought their own private wars. Including both anarchist and criminal elements, these groups might tread a narrow line between underground warfare and simple banditry.

Prison raids

Johannes Post, from the northern province of Drenthe, was a renowned Protestant LO-LKP leader who was involved in various parallel forms of resistance, including aiding Jews, forging documents, carrying out sabotage, and conducting raids. In summer 1944, determined to free a close friend and other political prisoners from an Amsterdam prison, Post prepared to mount a risky jail-break.

A Dutch prison guard and SS member named Jan Boogaard, who had previously served with the Waffen-SS on the Eastern Front, persuaded Post that he would be willing to perform an 'inside job' in return for the cleansing

---

E | **RESISTANCE, 1944–45**
(1) *Partizanenactie Nederland* **fighter; Eindhoven, September 1944**
The reconstruction is largely based on a photo of Theo van den Bogaard, a 23-year-old electrical engineer born near 's-Hertogenbosch. This Resistance fighter, already a KP veteran, was finally killed on 18 September 1944 while defending a post-office telephone exchange that the PAN had seized in Eindhoven, to coincide with Operation *Market Garden*. He wears entirely civilian clothing apart from his 'PAN/Oranje' brassard (see also Plate H5). His main weapon is a 6.5mm Hembrug (Dutch-made Mannlicher) M95 carbine. This shorter version of the M95 rifle, originally ordered for the police, was later also issued in the Army to cavalry, artillery, engineers, and liaison officers, and numbers of them found their way into Resistance hands following the May 1940 campaign. He has also tucked a captured German M24 stick grenade into his belt.
(2) *Stoottroepen* **soldier of ST Brabant Command; British Second Army, 1944–45**
The ST members who eventually formed the 15 companies (three battalions) of Brabant Command were initially described as looking like 'gypsies', but were later clothed, armed, equipped and trained by the British and Canadian armies. This *Stoter* has received a British Mk III 'turtle' helmet (in Dutch, *pannetje*, 'little pan'). On both sleeves of his 1940-pattern British 'economy' battledress he displays the white-on-black 'STOOTTROEPEN' shoulder title, above the Dutch national badge worn by Free Dutch and ST forces (see

also **2a & 2b**). He has basic British 37-pattern webbing equipment of belt, two munitions pouches and a water-bottle, and he is armed with an obsolescent .303in Ross Mk III rifle from Canadian stores. Dangerously, he also carries a couple of British No 36 fragmentation grenades ('Mills bombs') with the safety levers jammed over his belt.
(2a) ST shoulder title
(2b) Dutch national sleeve badge. These were made in light orange on uniform khaki, in handed pairs so that the lion could always face forwards.
(3) *Stoottroepen* **soldier of ST Limburg Command; US Ninth Army, 1944–45**
This *Stoter* serves in one of the 15 companies that were fully clothed in US Army issue: olive drab woollen shirt and trousers of light and dark shades respectively, an 'M1941' Parsons field jacket, M1938 canvas leggings, and brown 'rough-out' field shoes. Like the leggings, the M1923 rifle ammunition belt with attached M1942 first-aid pouch might be in either early khaki or greenish late-war OD shades. Behind his hip his belt would also support a canteen in its carrier. The orange-painted markings on his M1 steel hemet display his ST identity: a solid square on the front, and a stylized Dutch heraldic lion on the left side (see also **3a**). The wealth of insignia on his sleeve include the same shoulder title and national badge as **2**, above the shoulder-sleeve insignia of US Ninth Army: a white 'A' centred in a white quatrefoil, on a dark red disc. His weapon is a .30cal US Springfield M1903A4 rifle.
(3a) Dutch lion helmet marking

2a STOOTTROEPEN

1

2b NEDERLAND

2

3

3a

of his record. The raid took place on the night of 14/15 July 1944; it involved 16 KP fighters, of whom four remained outside on lookout. When Boogaard let the other 12 men through the gate, they were met by the SD: he had betrayed them from the start. After an exchange of fire six of the KP men, two of them wounded, were arrested. Johannes Post, who had not been present, was arrested the next day, and executed on 16 July in the Bloemendaal dunes – where, after the war, the remains of 422 executed Resistance members would be found. (Following the Liberation, Jan Boogaard would himself be put to death for treason.)

Another prison raid, but one which ended in spectacular success, was led by Piet Oberman (alias 'Piet Kramer'), the KP leader in the northern province of Friesland. On 8 December 1944, 25 KP members set out to raid a heavily guarded prison in the provincial capital, Leeuwarden. A devout Protestant, Oberman conducted group prayers before embarking on the mission with his carefully selected team. During thorough advance preparations, trustworthy prison guards had provided detailed information about the layout, the whereabouts of the prisoners to be rescued, and the character of fellow guards. The prison's telephone line had been tapped, and hiding-places for the freed prisoners had been organized beforehand. Six heavily armed men took up positions in a corner house overlooking two prison gateways. At the onset of the raid, an advance party of five KP men presented themselves at the prison's entrance, two of them disguised as police officers and the other three as 'arrested black-marketeers'. Once allowed entry, they overpowered the security staff and let 14 other raiders into the prison. The result was that no fewer than 51 prisoners were freed, without a single shot being fired.

OPEN WARFARE, FROM SEPTEMBER 1944

Establishment of the *Nederlandse Binnenlandse Strijdkrachten* (NBS, Netherlands Interior Forces)

On 3 September 1944, the Dutch government-in-exile announced over *Radio Oranje* that the OD, RVV and LKP were to be merged into an umbrella organization known as the Netherlands Interior Forces – the Dutch term also translates as 'Home Forces'. (In order to avoid confusion, readers should be careful hereafter not to mix up the NBS Interior Forces with the fascist NSB. In the Netherlands today, it is common to shorten 'NBS' to simply 'BS'.) It must be borne in mind that the NBS as an actual force was not established all at once. Some armed resistance groups continued to operate independently at a local level; they were absorbed into the NBS at different dates, and their previous titles often continued in use.

There were a number of reasons for the Dutch government-in-exile and the Resistance to establish the NBS. Firstly, there was a strong desire that the Dutch Resistance should actively participate in the Liberation, comparably to the example set by the *Forces française de l'intérieur* (FFI, French Interior Forces). Secondly, by moulding the three armed resistance organizations into a single structure subject to military discipline, the government-in-exile hoped to forestall extra-judicial killings as local groups exacted uncontrolled

(continued on page 42)

N

NORTH
SEA

Terschelling *Ameland* *Schiermonnikoog*

Vlieland

GRONINGEN

● Groningen

Texel

FRIESLAND

Leeuwarden ●

Afsluitdijk

● Assen

Westerbork △

DRENTHE

Schoorl △

Lake IJssel

Zwolle ● △ Ommen

NORTH
HOLLAND

OVERIJSSEL

Haarlem ●

□ AMSTERDAM

Deventer ○ Enschede ○

Apeldoorn ○

Amersfoort △

SOUTH
HOLLAND

UTRECHT

GELDERLAND

Zutphen ○

Den Haag ●
Delft ○

Utrecht ● Veenendaal ○

Wageningen ○ Arnhem ●

Rotterdam ○

Nijmegen ○

Waal

Biesbosch

Lower Rhine

ZEELAND

's-Hertogenbosch

Walcheren

Vught △ △
Haaren △ Sint-Michielsgestel

GERMANY

● Middelburg

Tilburg ○

Scheldt estuary

NORTH
BRABANT

Maas

○ Eindhoven

○ Venlo
○ Baarlo

ANTWERP ●

BELGIUM

LIMBURG

○ Roermond

Rhine

Heerlen ○

Maastricht ●

Key

□ capital city
● provincial capital
○ city, town or village
△ detention, transit, and/or concentration camp
━━ front line as of c.10 November 1944
── river
--- national boundary
······ provincial boundary

0 10 20 30 40 50 60 miles

ALLIED LIBERATION OPERATIONS, 1944–45

On 4 September 1944, as Field Marshal Montgomery's 21st Army Group – Second British Army (Gen Dempsey) and First Canadian Army (Gen Crerar) – pushed rapidly north-eastwards through western and central Belgium, the British 11th Armd Div entered the port-city of Antwerp, some 15 miles south of the Dutch border. However, since the Germans halted the division's advance on the Albert Canal just north of the city, it would be a US patrol, from the 117th Regimental Combat Team of Ninth Army's 30th Inf Div, who were the first Allied soldiers to enter the Netherlands – on 12 September, far to the south-east, near Maastricht in southern Limburg province. A few hours later, Mesch was the first Dutch village to be liberated, and by the 14th the city of Maastricht had been taken without opposition.

The failure of *Market Garden*
On 17 September, Montgomery launched his over-ambitious Operation *Market Garden*, the US/ British/ Polish airborne attempt to seize successive canal and river bridges, with the aim of allowing British XXX Corps to punch a corridor right up through North Brabant province into Gelderland, and across the Lower Rhine at Arnhem. Montgomery had persuaded Gen Eisenhower's Supreme Headquarters Allied Expeditionary Force (SHAEF) that this gamble was worth taking for the prize of opening a way for a right hook into Germany north of the Ruhr. While US 82nd Abn Div did secure the Waal river bridge at Nijmegen, and the British did liberate much of the eastern part of North Brabant, Arnhem – notoriously – proved to be 'a bridge too far' for British 1st Abn Div and their Polish comrades.

Following this failure, on 26 September 21st Army Group were left holding a concave front stretching roughly from Antwerp in the south-west to Nijmegen in the north-east, facing Gen von Zangen's German Fifteenth Army to the north. From the Nijmegen salient, the Allied eastern front – facing Gen Student's First Parachute Army – followed a wavering line southwards, up to 25 miles short of the north-south course of the Maas river.

In the aftermath of *Market Garden* Montgomery's forces were unbalanced, and seriously short of both supplies and logistic transport. Nevertheless, they faced the immediate necessity of clearing both south and north banks of the Scheldt estuary, in order to open the sea approaches to the vital port of Antwerp for Allied shipping, and meanwhile holding and expanding the Nijmegen salient.

The Maas front, October–November 1944
On that eastern front, the British operations *Aintree* and *Constellation* (from 30 September and 12 October respectively) took Overloon and Venray by 18 October, despite difficult ground and strong opposition; but the attack then stalled short of the Maas bend, when units were abruptly transferred to the priority Scheldt front. Operations *Mallard* and *Nutcracker* (from 14 and 19 November) faced the sodden Peel marshes, in bad weather which limited air support and against stiff resistance, but on 3 December the last German positions west of the Maas opposite Venlo were taken.

Zeeland and North Brabant, October–November 1944
From late September, Canadian and British operations had also begun on a broad front to the west and north: into Zeeland province to clear the Scheldt estuary, and up through west and central North Brabant. Hard fighting north of Antwerp saw Canadian troops capture Woensdrecht by 16 October. On the southern shore of the Scheldt estuary (Operation *Switchback*), the Canadians destroyed the German-held 'Breskens pocket' before the end of that month. Meanwhile, north of the estuary, they attacked up the South Beveland peninsula – a former island now linked by a causeway – on 21 October (Operation *Vitality*, and captured it in four days thanks to an amphibious landing behind the enemy's defensive line. In the mainly amphibious Operations *Infatuate I & II* (31 October–6 November), British and Canadian troops captured the flooded island of Walcheren, removing the threat of its heavy artillery (though at tragic cost in Dutch civilian lives). After lengthy mine-clearance, the first Allied supply ships docked in Antwerp on 28 November.

Further east, meanwhile, the north-westerly Operation *Pheasant* (20 October–4 November) drove German Fifteenth Army out of North Brabant between the Waal/Maas estuary and Nijmegen, with British and Canadian formations, 1st Polish Armd Div and US 104th Inf Div liberating Bergen-op-Zoom, Roosendaal, Breda, Tilburg and s'-Hertogenbosch (Den Bosch).

The 'Battle of the Bulge', December 1944–January 1945
In early December the junction of the British/Canadian and US armies was at Geilenkirchen between the Maas and Roer rivers in west Germany. In freezing winter weather, the Allied front remained largely inactive until 16 December – when the wholly unexpected German counter-offensive threw the weak US First Army front further south in the Ardennes into disarray, and monopolized SHAEF's attention for the next month. The Sixth SS Panzer, Fifth Panzer and Seventh armies struck north-westwards from the Eifel hills into Belgium, aiming for the Maas around Liège and eventually perhaps even Antwerp, to divide the British/Canadian 21st Army Group from Gen Omar Bradley's US 12th Army Group. Part of the Allied reaction, on 20 December, was to place Gen Hodges' US First and Gen Simpson's Ninth armies, which were north of the 35-mile wide German penetration, temporarily under Montgomery's command. West and south of 'the Bulge', Gen Bradley and Gen George Patton (US Third Army) would halt, defeat, and drive back the German offensive by mid-January.

The occupied northern and western Netherlands were not an Allied priority. Their cut-off German occupiers presented no real threat to SHAEF's immediate plans, which were to penetrate the 'Siegfried Line' and clear the Rhineland west of that river, and then to cross it and thrust on eastwards across Germany.

The Rhineland, January–March 1945
Having handed back US First Army to Gen Bradley, but retaining Ninth Army until late March, 21st Army Group first drove German Fifteenth Army out of the Maas–Roer triangle (Operation *Blackcock*, 16–26 January 1945). On 8 February, Montgomery launched First Canadian Army and British XXX Corps into Operation *Veritable*, south-eastwards from a front about 30 miles south-east of Nijmegen. This involved fighting through both forested and partially flooded terrain, to take prepared defences and stubbornly defended towns, driving Gen Schlemm's First Parachute Army out of the Reichswald forest and off the sodden plains west of the Rhine. From 23 February this operation was supported by US Ninth Army's eastwards Operation *Grenade* further south; Venlo and Roermond were taken on 1 March, and the two Allied thrusts met around Wesel on the Rhine on 3 March.

The costly Canadian Operation *Blockbuster* (26 February–10 March) finally brought enemy resistance on the west bank to an end. The successful Rhine crossings at Wesel and Rees (Operation *Plunder*) followed from 23/24 March, after which Ninth Army reverted to US command.

The central and north-eastern provinces, April–May 1945

During January–February 1945 the Canadian I Corps (Gen Charles Foulkes) had been transported up from Italy to join II Corps (Gen Guy Simonds) in NW Europe. After hard fighting for Emmerich in the north of the Rhine bridgehead (28–30 March), at the beginning of April the reinforced Canadian First Army (with some attached British elements, notably 49th Inf Div) finally advanced both westwards and northwards to liberate the Dutch central and north-eastern provinces. To limit civilian casualties as much as possible, some urban attacks had to be made without heavy artillery or air support.

On 2 April the British 49th Inf Div captured the waterlogged 'island' between Nijmegen and Arnhem. During 2–8 April, II Canadian Corps took Zutphen and Deventer on the east bank of the IJssel river. Both corps then crossed the IJssel westwards (11 and 12 April). In Gelderland during 14–16 April, 49th Inf Div occupied the ruins of Arnhem (Operation *Anger*), and 1st Cdn Inf

Div from I Corps took the harder objective of Apeldoorn (Operation *Cannonshot*). Far to the north, on 15 April 3rd Cdn Inf Div from II Corps took Leeuwarden, capital of Friesland, and the following day its 2nd Inf Div secured another provincial capital, Groningen, in hard street fighting. On 17 April a counterattack in Otterlo, Gelderland, by an encircled German unit was beaten off in close-quarter fighting by I Corps troops of 5th Armoured Division.

On 19 April orders arrived shifting II Cdn Corps eastwards, to cover the left flank of British Second Army during its dash for Hamburg and the Baltic coast east of Denmark. By this date SHAEF had decided not to assault into the western provinces of 'Old Holland' beyond Lake IJssel, for humanitarian reasons: they offered no strategic objectives, they were crowded with starving civilians after the 'Hunger Winter', and a German surrender was obviously imminent. On 5 May, in the *De Wereld* ('The World') hotel, at Wageningen in Gelderland, the I Cdn Corps GOC Gen Foulkes received the surrender of all German forces in the Netherlands from Gen Blaskowitz, C-in-C North-West, in the presence of Prince Bernhard.

Sources:
Robert Buckley, *Monty's Men* (Yale University Press, 2013)
Terry Copp, *Cinderella Army* (University of Toronto Press, 2006)

26 February 1945, the first day of Operation *Blockbuster*: Canadian infantrymen of the Algonquin Regt, from 10th Inf Bde, 4th Cdn Armd Div, II Corps, ride on Sherman tanks of the South Alberta Regt on their way towards the Hochwald Gap. *Blockbuster* was the last phase of Operation *Veritable* to capture the territory between the rivers Maas and Rhine; it would cost more than 8,000 Allied casualties, but would inflict three times that many on the Wehrmacht. (Library & Archives of Canada, PA113907)

revenge on (perceived) collaborators. Many resistance fighters had been living like outlaws throughout the Occupation, committing acts that would be inadmissible under normal circumstances, and the government was anxious that they should not spiral out of control when the Netherlands threw off its German shackles. Thirdly, as the armed Resistance presented a more formally identified appearance under the banner of the NBS, the government hoped that captured resistance fighters might be treated by the Germans as legitimate combatants rather than 'terrorists' or 'bandits'. In the event, in both the second and third of these hopes, the government was to be disappointed.

Prince Bernhard of Lippe-Biesterfeld, the German-born husband of Queen Wilhelmina's daughter Crown Princess Juliana, acted in Great Britain as the chief liaison officer between SHAEF and the Dutch government-in-exile. He was now appointed by his mother-in-law as the overall commander of the NBS, though as far as can be ascertained this command was largely symbolic in nature. The three commanders of the OD, RVV and LKP constituted a triumvirate known as the 'Delta Triangle'. This was headed by a commander operating in the occupied part of the Netherlands named Henri Koot. Hailing from the Dutch East Indies (present-day Indonesia), and having a white Dutch father and an ethnic Chinese mother, Koot had previously served as a colonel in the *Koninklijk Nederlands-Indisch Leger* (KNIL – see MAA 521, *Royal Netherlands East Indies Army 1936–42*).

Koot regarded himself as a referee between the three resistance organizations, which were somewhat at odds with one another, but in practice

---

F RESISTANCE, 1945

(1) University student member, NBS; Delft, May 1945

This student in Delft, a university city in the western province of South Holland, has only emerged as a member of the NBS after the German surrender of 5 May. Nevertheless, he is armed with a British .303in Lee Enfield No 1 Mk III rifle and is alert for action, since Canadian troops were slow to reach this region and disarm the German garrison and local fascists. With his rather *'sportif '* civilian clothes he wears a black-painted Dutch M34 steel helmet, and carries ammunition and small kit in a captured German bread-bag. The vertically-striped tricolour NBS brassard was characteristic of this city (see also Plate **H3**). Note the white carnation on his left lapel; this, Prince Bernhard's favourite flower, was a symbol of wartime defiance. Nowadays the white carnation is worn to express appreciation for Dutch war-dead and veterans, much as the red poppy is displayed in Great Britain.

During the Occupation many students were active in all forms of resistance, including espionage and armed missions. The national consultative body of students, the *Raad van Negen* ('Council of Nine'), coordinated these activities. From 1943 onwards the occupying forces required all students to sign a pledge of loyalty renouncing any anti-German activity. The vast majority who refused to sign – both male and female – were expelled from their universities and had to report for forced labour, being transferred to the Erika concentration camp near Ommen. Those who did not report usually had to go into hiding, continuing their resistance work among the 'submerged' population.

(2) Order Service member, NBS; Heerlen, February 1945

This figure is partly based on an OD member photographed in Heerlen, a city north-east of Maastricht in southern Limburg. His black-painted M34 helmet bears 'O.D.' painted in orange; although the OD, RVV and LKP were officially merged into the NBS in early September 1944, pre-existing affiliations continued to be acknowledged locally. Like many other OD members, this neatly turned-out volunteer has a Dutch Army background; his leather-reinforced grey riding breeches and spurred riding boots suggest previous service in the *Korps Rijdende Artillerie* (KRA, Horse Artillery Corps), nicknamed the *Gele Rijders* or 'Yellow Riders'. Below the usual 'ORANJE' his brassard bears a blue salamander symbol (see also under Plate **H6**). The orange ribbon bow on the lapel of his grey tweed civilian jacket is a mark of loyalty to the Dutch royal family (the House of Orange-Nassau). His impressive war booty consists of a German Fallschirmjäger helmet and an FG42 paratrooper's assault rifle. Following British XII Corps' Operation *Blackcock* in the Roer triangle north of Heerlen (16-26 January), paratroop patrols from Kampfgruppe Hübner often probed the new front line.

(3) NBS fighter, eastern or northern provinces, April 1945

When the NBS in the eastern and northern provinces rose to fight in April 1945, many members simply wore workers' blue overalls and a black alpine beret (as used, for instance, by the Dutch National Bn in Gelderland). This fighter has also acquired a pair of German 'dice-shaker' marching boots. He wears the plainest type of NBS brassard (see also Plate **H1**), and sports a cockade in the Dutch national colours on his chest. Having raided a German arsenal, he is more heavily armed than most of his comrades, with an 8.8cm reloadable anti-tank rocket projector. This Raketenpanzerbüchse (RPzB) was nicknamed the 'Panzerschreck' (roughly, 'tank-terror'), but was equally effective against defended buildings.

North Brabant province was the scene of much fighting during the Allied advance in October 1944. Here an NBS-affiliated policeman of the *Marechaussee* (left) and an NBS motorcycle courier (right) interrogate a captured German soldier. Judging by his camouflage jacket and baggy khaki Luftwaffe summer trousers, he seems to be a Feldjäger from a Luftwaffe Feld-Division. (Beeldbankwo2.nl/ NIOD)

the OD had the strongest influence on him. With the knowledge of Prince Bernhard, Koot introduced a centralized command structure, within which he gave perhaps excessive authority to the OD faction. This exacerbated its quarrels with the LKP and the RVV. As mentioned above, the RVV were (incorrectly) perceived by many conservatives as essentially leftist revolutionaries. The right wing of the Dutch Resistance genuinely feared that Communist elements were plotting to seize state power by force of arms after the German surrender (as would be attempted, for instance, in Greece, leading to the Civil War of 1946–49). The other groups, in their turn, were wary of the OD, which had previously been infiltrated by German security (see above, 'The England Game'), and which now sought to monopolize positions of authority within the NBS.

At the outset the capacity of the NBS was limited, numbering about 6,800 men in September 1944, of which 4,000 came from the OD, 1,800 from the LKP, and 1,000 from the RVV. The NBS were divided into a *Strijdend Gedeelte* (SG, 'Combat Wing'), and a 'Guard Section' known as *Bewakingstroepen* (BT). The latter were to maintain public order, arrest NSB members, and guard vital locations such as road junctions and bridges. Only those who were willing and able to fight the Nazis in the front line were allowed to serve in the combat wing of the NBS. Obviously, this SG was initially formed with LKP and RVV members who already had a track-record of fighting Germans and collaborators, while the guard duties would fall more naturally to the OD.

However, when it turned out that for manpower reasons the NBS combat battalions could not be filled with LKP and RVV members alone, OD men were also admitted. It should be noted that the boundary between combat and guard duties within the NBS was sometimes blurred. In practice, some guard companies found themselves engaged in combat, whereas some combat sections were tasked with guarding prisoners. In many cases, which roles were played by individual combat and guard companies on the ground depended very much on local circumstances.

Later on, recruits with no previous Resistance background were also accepted into the NBS. The first wave of newcomers joined up in September 1944 when the Allies liberated the southern half of the Netherlands, and German defeat seemed to be imminent. The war-seasoned Resistance veterans referred to these newcomers as *Septemberartiesten* ('September artists') or *Septembervliegen* ('September flies').

Operation *Market Garden* and its aftermath

In an attempt to end the war by Christmas 1944, the British FM Montgomery had conceived an ambitious plan which came to be known as Operation

Market Garden. His aim was to create a salient into occupied Dutch territory, which in turn could serve as an invasion route into the Ruhr, Germany's industrial heartland. This was to be achieved by airborne forces securing a series of strategic canal and river bridges, with armour and infantry following up swiftly to relieve the paras and cross the seized bridges. The US 101st Airborne Division was tasked with securing bridges near Son and Veghel in the southern province of North Brabant. The US 82nd Abn Div was to take the bridges over the Maas and Waal rivers near Grave (North Brabant) and Nijmegen (Gelderland). The British 1st Abn Div, plus the Polish 1st Independent Para Bde, was ordered to take the Lower Rhine bridge in Arnhem (Gelderland). XXX Corps of British Second Army was tasked with advancing to and over these key bridges to consolidate the salient. Famously, in the event the final objective could not be secured, since

Joyful members of the Netherlands Interior Forces in Breda, North Brabant province, celebrate the liberation of their city in October 1944. The fighter on the left carries a captured German MG34, his comrade a stick grenade and spare 'link' for the MG; note that he wears his tricolour brassard around his lower arm. (Getty Images)

the ground forces failed to relieve in time the hard-pressed British para- and glider-troopers at Arnhem (17–25 September 1944).

In preparation for *Market Garden*, in September 1944 the Dutch government-in-exile had called for an all-out railway strike in order to obstruct German military movements. More than 30,000 employees of the *Nederlandse Spoorwegen* (NS, Netherlands Railways) responded to the call, and simply went into hiding. As in spring 1943, the reprisals were extreme: Reichskommissar Seyss-Inquart declared a 'state of siege', and, apart from launching the predictable manhunts and firing squads, he ceased all food and fuel supplies to the occupied western provinces. This initiated the desperate 'Hunger Winter' of 1944/45, which saw some 20,000 civilian deaths from starvation and disease among the hungry and freezing population.

In the run-up to *Market Garden* the resistance organizations focused on sabotage, in particular of the railways. From 3 September 1944 onwards the main rail lines were cut, and in those two weeks prior to the airborne landings there was a permanent blockage of rail traffic in the German-held areas. The Resistance also initiated various other operations to assist or coincide with the Allied advance.

'The forest partisans of Baarlo'
For instance, three KPs converged in the woods around Baarlo, a village near Venlo in Limburg province, with the aim of both protecting vital buildings and cutting railways. The KPs involved came from Schijndel (a town in North Brabant); from a region between the Maas and Waal rivers in Gelderland; and from the northern part of Limburg. In total, this force numbered 29 fighters. Since the Limburg KP, under the overall command of Jacques Crasborn, was in desperate need of weapons, it was decided to target small groups of Germans in order to acquire them.

On 14 September 1944, the highly motivated KP fighters took their first prisoners, numbering four war-weary middle-aged Germans. In total, the group would capture nearly 30 Germans, including 11 paratroopers (and with them, 16 Panzerfaust anti-tank weapons). Holding so many prisoners proved to be a serious burden for the small Resistance party. Hunted by the Germans, they and their PoWs constantly had to relocate to different makeshift shelters in cold, rainy weather, and morale suffered. Matters came to a climax when two captured 'deserters' turned out to be Austrian SS-men, who tried to infiltrate the KP group and to rouse the other prisoners against their captors; both these men were executed on 2 October.

Finally, on 19 November 1944, after a hazardous ordeal lasting 66 days, the group established contact with soldiers of 154th Inf Bde from the British 51st (Highland) Inf Div, and handed over their prisoners. Subsequently, the KP fighters – clad in khaki overalls or captured German camouflage jackets – guided the British troops through the Baarlo woods, and helped to carry in their wounded under enemy shell-fire. These KP fighters became renowned as the *bospartizanen van Baarlo* ('forest partisans of Baarlo'), but their legacy remains disputed. Some praise them for pulling off a courageous feat, while others argue that they recklessly exposed themselves and the local community to unnecessary risks. Some of the KP members, Crasborn included, subsequently joined the *Stoottroepen* (Shock Forces – see below).

Partizanenactie Nederland
(PAN. Partisan Action Netherlands)

Another armed resistance organization that sought to assist the Allied advance in September 1944 was this group operating in the area of Eindhoven, a city in North Brabant. By August 1944 the PAN numbered approximately 600 men. In early September it started to sabotage the railways in order to frustrate the Wehrmacht's logistics. On the night of 17/18 September the PAN embarked on open warfare, seizing objectives, capturing German soldiers and NSB members, and losing 12 of their own killed in the process. In addition, the PAN helped units of US 101st Abn Div and British Guards Armd Div by pointing out German positions. On 23 September the PAN was absorbed into the ST (again, see below).

At the bridges

In Nijmegen the Germans had attached explosives to the Waal bridge, an objective of US 82nd Airborne Division. It is generally believed that Jan van Hoof, a 22-year-old student, successfully neutralized the explosives on 18 September, thus saving the bridge from demolition. A member of the espionage organization *Geheime Dienst Nederland* (Secret Service Netherlands), Van Hoof had carefully reconnoitered the bridge in advance. The next day he was killed while guiding a British vehicle in Nijmegen city.

During the battle of Arnhem, a few hundred resistance members served alongside the Allies as either guides or combatants. Their orange brassards failed to convince the Germans that these irregular volunteers were legitimate combatants, and when the Wehrmacht recaptured the Arnhem bridge and the village of Oosterbeek, Waffen-SS veterans of fighting in the East and in France executed any fighters they captured.

The Biesbosch

By November 1944 the front line in the Netherlands had more or less stalled, cutting the country into an occupied North and a liberated South (see map, page 39). This front roughly followed the course of the great rivers, and in this context the Biesbosch region, situated in the Waal/ Maas estuary on the boundary between the two zones, became a lifeline.

The Biesbosch is an extensive tidal freshwater area, forming a labyrinth of rivers, creeks and reedbeds which provided a haven for people in hiding and for Resistance members. The Germans understood this, but, being unfamiliar with the difficult terrain, they hesitated to venture into the Biesbosch. From November 1944 until May 1945, 21 so-called 'line-crossers' would smuggle Jewish refugees, shot-down Allied aircrew, couriers and intelligence from the occupied North through the Biesbosch to the liberated South, and bring back secret agents and medical supplies. These crossings were made by rowingboat or canoe, covering distances of 8–11 miles (13–18km). They were a dangerous undertaking, and two of the line-crossers did not survive the war. In total, 374 return trips were made. One of the people who was spirited from the north to the south was Brig John 'Shan' Hackett, commander of the British 4th Para Bde, who had been seriously wounded during the fighting for Arnhem.

Another remarkable feat was the capture of 75 German prisoners by the local KP in the Biesbosch. On 5 November 1944 this group, which included a number of Poles, Italians and Dutch SS-men, was successfully ferried to the south and handed over to Gen Maczek's Polish 1st Armoured Division.

Enter the *Stoottroepen* (ST, Shock Forces)

As mentioned above, when the Allies liberated the southern Netherlands in September 1944, local Resistance members emerged to fight alongside them. Earning credibility and practical Allied support, some NBS groups in the liberated South acquired the organization, equipment and appearance of a regular force. The NBS in the occupied North, meanwhile, necessarily remained underground, and only embarked on open warfare in April 1945 when the Allies resumed their advance. Thus the northern NBS retained their irregular and improvised character until the very end of the war, while some of their southern compatriots were transformed into regular soldiers.

The term *Stoottroepen* (ST) can be understood as 'Shock Forces'; an individual ST member was referred to as a *Stoter* (plural: *Stoters*). In the southern province of Limburg the *Stoottroepen Regiment Limburg* or Limburg Command came into existence with American support. Led by LO-LKP veteran Bep van Kooten, it became an integral part of Gen Simpson's US Ninth Army. The Americans quickly deployed the Shock Troops along the front line, tasking them with patrolling and reconnaissance. On 12 October 1944, the first Limburg Command *Stoter* was killed east of Nieuwstadt while leading a reconnaissance patrol; his name was Theo Dautzenberg, and he was posthumously awarded the US Silver Star. Eventually the Limburg Command mustered three battalions totalling 15 companies, of which three joined the Americans in their crossing of the Rhine; they ended up deep inside Germany, reaching the cities of Paderborn, Brunswick, Oschersleben and Magdeburg. Once on German soil the Limburg *Stoters* were mainly tasked with guarding and policing duties, including supervising military convoys.

Wim Schreur went into hiding to avoid forced labour for the Germans. When the southern part of Limburg province was liberated in September 1944 he reported for duty in the Netherlands Interior Forces, and subsequently served in the *Stoottroepen* of Limburg Command with US Ninth Army. Note the orange square and the lion motif on his M1 helmet (see Plate E3 & 3a). While taking part in a reconnaissance mission east of Nieuwstadt, Schreur narrowly escaped death when a sniper's bullet ricocheted off his weapon. (NIMH)

The two central figures represent two different segments within the armed Dutch Resistance from autumn 1944. On the left is an NBS commander, wearing an improvised mixture of military and civilian clothing, including a Dutch Army sidecap and a white-striped black NBS command patch on his right lapel. He is talking to a *Stoter* of the ST (Shock Forces) Limburg Command, wearing complete US Army uniform. On his left sleeve the latter displays the insignia illustrated on Plate E: the 'STOOTTROEPEN' shoulder title, 'NEDERLAND' national lion sleeve badge, and US Ninth Army shoulder-sleeve insignia. (NIMH)

ST soldiers of Limburg Command photographed in Visé, a Belgian town just across the Netherlands border from that province. The soldier on the left wears British 1940-pattern battledress, although armed with a US .30cal M1 carbine. His two comrades are in US Army uniform with the full suite of insignia on their left sleeves; the central man has an M3 shoulder holster with cartridge loops attached. (NIMH)

Meanwhile, in North Brabant and Zeeland the British and Canadians helped to establish the *Stoottroepen Regiment Brabant* or Brabant Command. Also numbering 15 companies, this became part of Gen Miles Dempsey's British Second Army. The KPs in the south-western province of Zeeland were too few in number to form a Command of their own, but an ST company from Zeeland was assigned to the Brabant Command. The Brabant ST were deployed along the southern banks of the Waal and Maas rivers, with the main task of preventing German scouting and raiding parties from the occupied North penetrating into the liberated South.

Initially, the ST had to fend for themselves in terms of weaponry, clothing and food, and might turn out for duty carrying captured German weapons but wearing worn-out civilian clothes and shod in wooden *klompen* ('clogs'). When Gen Simpson saw members of the Limburg Command for the first time, he is said to have remarked: 'What an army!....', while a similar encounter prompted a British officer in North Brabant to describe them as 'gypsies'. From mid-November 1944 onwards, however, the ST were clothed, equipped, armed and fed from regular American, British and Canadian stores. There were also a number of women among the ST, who were given non-combat roles such as nurses, typists and couriers.

In total, some 6,000 ST members are believed to have served between September 1944 and May 1945, of whom 102 were killed in action (though another source gives figures of 4,000 and 260 respectively). General Dempsey characterized the North Brabant *Stoters* as 'F***ing good fighters, but a little too crazy'. Driven by a strong desire to help liberate their country, the ST proved to be brave in battle (five men of the Limburg Command were awarded the US Bronze Star), but their eagerness to get at the Germans sometimes made it difficult to enforce military discipline.

In January 1945 the Limburg Command was absorbed into the newly founded *Koninklijke Landmacht* (KL, Royal Land Force – the reborn Dutch Army), whereas the Brabant Command was assigned to the KL only in May 1945.

THE RENEWED ALLIED ADVANCE, MARCH–APRIL 1945

Woeste Hoeve

In the night of 6/7 March 1945, the NBS group from Apeldoorn, a city in Gelderland, staged an ambush near Woeste Hoeve, a hamlet between Apeldoorn and Arnhem. The group, which included two Austrian Waffen-SS deserters, had intended to capture a German lorry. However, when vehicles stopped at their makeshift checkpoint, one turned out to be SS-Ogruf Rauter's BMW staff car. In the shoot-out that followed, two passengers were killed and the HSSPF himself was wounded, though he survived by 'playing dead' until rescued.

Allied soldiers, almost certainly Scots from 52nd (Lowland) Inf Div, photographed with resistance fighters in Vlissingen (Flushing), a port-town in Zeeland province, shortly after the successful conclusion of the battle for the Scheldt estuary in November 1944. During this hard two-month campaign, Dutch scouts provided Allied troops with valuable intelligence about German dispositions, and on some occasions fought alongside them. (Beeldbank Zeeland)

The Germans responded with their greatest mass shooting of the Occupation, executing 263 people in all. Some of the victims were rounded up in the vicinity, and the rest were political prisoners and Resistance members already in custody elsewhere; these included 'Long John' Thijssen, co-founder of the RVV. [6]

SAS operations

When the Allies resumed their advance in March–April 1945, various areas in the central Netherlands became the focus of Special Air Service operations, which were assisted by local Resistance groups.

6 Put on trial for war crimes by a Dutch court in 1948, Rauter was executed by firing squad on 24 March 1949.

A *Stoter* of the British-equipped Brabant Command (see Plate E2) receiving range training with a .303in Ross Mk III rifle from a second lieutenant of 8th Bn, Middlesex Regt, the machine-gun battalion of 43rd (Wessex) Infantry Division. (NIMH)

This photo shows an NBS member named Hans van Douwe guiding French–Canadian soldiers of the *Régiment de la Chaudière* from 8th Inf Bde, 3rd Cdn Inf Div in Zutphen, a city astride the IJssel river dividing Overijssel and Gelderland provinces. After other divisional elements had broken in with the support of Shermans and Churchill flame-thrower tanks, 8th Bde spent 7–8 April 1945 clearing the streets of stubborn defenders. Van Douwe carries a rifle taken from a German arsenal. (Zutphen Municipality)

In Drenthe province in early 1945, the *Marechaussee* police officer Dirk Stoel (left, and compare Plate G1) sheltered in his home the Dutch commando Sgt Willem van der Veer (right) – who himself had served in that corps in May 1940 – when he was parachuted in to provide weapons-training to resistance fighters. Wim van der Veer had already operated behind Japanese lines in Burma; in April 1945 he would link up with Free French paratroopers during Operation *Amherst*, to neutralize GenMaj Karl Böttger's command centre at Westerbork. (Private photo, unknown wartime source; courtesy Jan Bruggink)

In December 1944 a group of about 30 young Dutchmen were flown from the liberated provinces to Great Britain to be trained by the SAS. Some of them were military veterans of the May 1940 campaign; some had been in the Resistance, or had otherwise assisted the Allied advance in the South. They entered service with the *Bureau Bijzondere Opdrachten* (BBO, Special Assignments Bureau), a new secret unit created by the government-in-exile in the spring of 1944. About 15 of the recruits successfully completed the demanding training programme, which included parachuting, extreme jeep-driving, handling of weapons and explosives, and silent killing.

The men who passed this course participated in Operation *Keystone*, an SAS mission that took place in early April 1945 in the Veluwe region. Its objective was to secure a number of bridges over the IJssel river, to enable Canadian I Corps units to cross from east to west. Additionally, it was intended that *Keystone* should create chaos behind the German lines in cooperation with the Dutch Resistance, permitting the Allies to advance more easily into the central Netherlands. (One of the secondary objectives was to capture or assassinate Reichskommissar Seyss-Inquart at his villa in Apeldoorn, but intelligence reports that he was absent at the time put paid to this scheme.)

For various reasons *Keystone* did not go according to plan, mainly because some air-drops of both soldiers and weapons went adrift. The operation was thus reduced to a number of acts of sabotage committed by an SAS foot party led by Capt Richard Holland near Nijkerk, Putten and Voorthuizen; and separate actions by an SAS jeep party led by Maj Henry Druce, which broke through the German lines at Arnhem and attacked enemy troops just behind the front.

More successful in part was the almost simultaneous Operation *Amherst*, by members of two French SAS units in adjoining areas of Drenthe, Groningen and Friesland provinces. (In December 1943 the Free French *2e & 3e Régiments de Chasseurs Parachutistes* had been incorporated into the SAS with 'parallel identities' as the 4th and 3rd SAS Regts respectively.) On the night of 7/8 April more than 700 of these paras, divided into 47 'sticks' of 15 men each, landed in the northern Netherlands. Their mission was to secure important road intersections and bridges to smooth the advance of Canadian II Corps units. In this they were assisted by local NBS forces often operating as independent KPs. Some of the drops were badly scattered, so separate parties of paras carried out their missions with varying degrees of success.

On 9 April, one stick made contact with a jeep party of the Belgian 5th SAS Regiment. These Belgians had been deployed a few days earlier, on 5 April, as part of Operation *Larkswood*, with the mission of reconnaissance and flank-screening on the left of units of 21st Army Group. With the support of local NBS groups, Belgian jeep parties cleared roadblocks; captured an important bridge at Oosterhesselen for the advancing Polish 1st Armd Div; and mopped up remaining German pockets. In total, 33 French SAS paras were killed in action or summarily executed when captured, while the Belgian SAS lost six men. More than 90 Dutch nationals were killed – some of them fighters who fell in action, and others resisters and civilians executed for having (actually or allegedly) assisted the SAS.

These three NBS members wearing mainly civilian clothing were photographed in spring 1945 in Groenlo, a city in Gelderland province, where they were tasked with guarding German PoWs and NSB members. The man on the left is H. Lansink, a veteran of the May 1940 campaign. (Courtesy Willy Lansink)

Dutch National Battalion (DNB)

As the Allies rapidly liberated the eastern provinces of Gelderland and Overijssel and the northern provinces of Drenthe, Friesland and Groningen, the NBS created an additional unit. This 'Dutch National Battalion' (DNB – surprisingly, no Dutch-language title appears in the sources) was formed on 15 April 1945 in the liberated municipality of Aalten in Gelderland. It mustered three companies each of about 130 men from the LKP, RVV and OD, supplemented by numbers of the 'submerged' who now emerged from hiding, eager to contribute to the Liberation. Initially dressed in the Dutch worker's ubiquitous blue overalls and black berets, identified by orange brassards and mostly armed with captured weapons, they would eventually

Group photo of the NBS group in Raalte, a town in Overijssel province, posing with a motorcycle captured from the local *Landwacht*. Most wear the Dutch M34 helmet, and are identified as members of the combat wing of the NBS by 'SG' brassards (compare with Plate H4). Most are armed with Sten SMGs, but one brandishes a 2.36in M1 anti-tank rocket launcher; this US 'bazooka' was one of the most powerful types of weapon supplied by the Allies. (Historische Vereniging Raalte en Omstreken)

During April 1945 the British 49th (West Riding) Inf Div, originally formed in Yorkshire, was subordinated to Canadian I Corps for the liberation of the eastern and central Netherlands. Here a sergeant of an unidentified unit of the division (though his gauntlets suggest he is a motorcyclist), displays its polar bear shoulder patch. He confers with a middle-aged NBS commander wearing a Dutch Army sidecap, and displaying a lapel rank patch and a brassard – compare with Plate G2. (NIMH)

be dressed, armed and, as far as possible, trained by Canadian I Corps, of which they became an integral part. The DNB helped to protect the flank of the Canadian and British troops during their advance in the Veluwe area of Gelderland, where it also assisted in mopping up pockets of German resistance, and guarded the boundary between liberated and occupied territory in early May 1945.

G | NETHERLANDS INTERIOR FORCES

(1) *Wachtmeester, Marechaussee*, September 1944 onwards
This police sergeant's affiliation to the Resistance is indicated by an orange brassard, faintly lettered in black 'ORDEDIENST' above a circular authentication stamp of his municipality (this example is from Harderwijk in northern Gelderland). The black kepi has royal-blue piping around the crown and both edges of the band, and an oval-shaped orange cockade edged with silver thread is secured by a silver-cord loop to a white-metal button bearing the flaming-grenade emblem (as do all buttons on this uniform). The double-breasted black cotton tunic has a royal-blue standing collar, two rows of seven buttons, and no exterior pockets. The striking distinction of the *Marechausse* corps is the triple aiguillettes of white goat-hair, with plaited shoulder cords of the same material. On both forearms a white reversed chevron of 'scooped' shape, edged with royal-blue piping, indicates the rank of *Wachtmeester*. The royal-blue riding breeches are worn with black riding boots. His black 'Sam Browne'-type belt supports an M1876/95 No 1 sabre with an orange-tasselled black fist-strap, and a single ammunition pouch for his 6.5mm Hembrug carbine.

(2) NBS commander, September 1944 onwards
This quite 'regular'-looking local commander is based on photos kindly provided by the National Military Museum at Soesterberg. With his civilian clothing he is wearing British-supplied khaki denim tank overalls, and a blue-grey ('field grey') prewar Dutch Army sidecap. The rank distinctions of NBS commanders were worn on single or paired black collar or lapel patches, but the exact grade identified by this single white bar is unconfirmed. Insignia displayed on his left sleeve (see also **2a**) begin with a shoulder title, lettered 'NEDERLAND' in blue on a blue-piped rectangular orange strip. The square orange patch below this, lettered 'STRIJDEND/ GEDEELTE' (often abbreviated to 'SG'), indicates the combat wing of the NBS. He has cut up a tricolour brassard and sewed or glued a section to his sleeve (see note under Plate **H2**). He carries a holstered 9mm FN Browning semi-automatic pistol.

(3) NBS motorcycle courier; Friesland, May 1945
This motorcyclist is participating in one of the province's many victory parades; in the local Frisian language the Netherlands Interior Forces were termed the *Nederlânske Binnenltânske Striidkrêften*. He wears captured German goggles over a brown leather flying helmet, and a three-quarter length black leather coat over commonplace blue overalls. His role is identified by 'ORDONANS' ('orderly') on his tricolour brassard, and for the occasion he sports an orange sash to display his loyalty to the Dutch royal family. His machine is a captured German DKW NZ350. The orange plate on the front mudguard is lettered 'NBS Gew. I ', which is short for *Gewest I* ('Sub-region 1'); Friesland was the first of the ten sub-regions into which the NBS were divided. Above this is attached, on an orange rod, a Frisian flag. The small red motifs on this proud expression of regional identity are commonly mistaken for hearts, but are in fact stylized *pompebleden* (waterlily leaves).

1

2

2a

STRIJDEND

GEDEELTE

ORANJE

3

NBS Gew. I

Captain Arie Meijer (centre), initially the OD commander and subsequently the overall NBS commander in Friesland province, flanked by two of his comrades. At first there was no love lost between the OD and KP factions, but the politically liberal Meijer achieved a fruitful cooperation between them, and then liberated almost the whole province before the arrival of Canadian units. For these achievements Capt Meijer was awarded the US Order of Merit by SHAEF. (Beeldbankwo2.nl/ NIOD & Fries Verzetsmuseum)

Surrounded by Friesland NBS members in improvised clothing typical of the northern provinces, the slightly-built Free Dutch agent Nicholaas de Koning (centre) stands out in the British Parachute Regt's maroon beret, a 37-pattern battledress blouse with his 'wings' worn on the left breast, and 43-pattern 'trousers, parachutist'. A veteran of a No.10 (IA) Cdo detachment to the Arakan front, Niek de Koning was credited with the underground training of up to 1,500 Resistance fighters in Friesland before the uprising of 14 April 1945. (Beeldbankwo2.nl/ NIOD & Fries Verzetsmuseum)

THE LIBERATION OF FRIESLAND

The liberation of Friesland province provides an interesting case-study in the contribution made by the NBS to the final Allied advance. In mid-April 1945 the NBS forces in Friesland liberated almost the entire province save for a few German pockets, paving the way for the advancing Canadians so successfully that the commander of their 3rd Inf Div would write that 'Friesland liberated herself'. Those German pockets were in Harlingen, a port in the north-western corner of the province; in the villages of Pingjum and Makkum; and at the entrance to the Afsluitdijk ('Enclosure Dam'), the long causeway connecting Friesland with the western province of North Holland and separating the freshwater Lake IJssel from the sea. The NBS naturally lacked the mortars and artillery required to dislodge these remaining enemy strongholds, but did succeed in isolating them.

This success was by no means an easy task to accomplish. The establishment of the provincial NBS had required a merger between the OD and KP (the RVV had no significant presence there), and there was the usual mutual mistrust and antipathy between the OD and KP factions in Friesland. Having a considerable number of ex-Army officers, the local OD believed it had the necessary military expertise to take the lead. Equally predictably, the KP cited their long record of active resistance as supporting their claim for the most influential positions within the new NBS. Eventually, Capt Arie Meijer, who headed the OD in Friesland, would become the overall commander of the provincial NBS, while KP leader Piet

Oberman (leader of the successful prison raid in Leeuwarden) would command a 'sabotage wing'. Oberman's deputy was former policeman Toon Alderliesten, a KP veteran whose conscience had led him to leave the *Marechaussee* during the spring 1943 general strike. For the sake of cohesion, from the moment of the merger onwards the terms 'OD' and 'KP' were no longer allowed to be used.

The NBS forces in Friesland were divided between 11 operational districts. Versions of their total numerical strength vary slightly, from 2,000 combat troops and 200 saboteurs, to 2,750 combat troops and 250 saboteurs. Prior to the liberation campaign in April 1945, many of these volunteers had received weapons-training from a parachuted-in Free Dutch former commando, Nicholaas (Niek) de Koning, who had previously taken part in a reconnaissance mission in Burma (present-day Myanmar). Masquerading as a veterinarian or a livestock-trader, under various aliases including 'Arie Prins', De Koning had travelled from place to place in Friesland, instructing as many as 1,500 underground troops.

In his headquarters in Leeuwarden, SS-Hstuf Wilhelm Artur Albrecht, head of the SD in Friesland, was aware that an underground force was being established. Not knowing that his telephone line was tapped by the Resistance, he was heard pondering how and when this secret army would reveal itself. His answer came on 14 April 1945, when the NBS in Friesland embarked on open warfare. The ensuing engagements were too numerous to describe in full here, but the following three examples are representative.

In Blauwverlaat, a hamlet near Achtkarspelen in the eastern part of Friesland, an NBS group commanded by a civil servant named Willem van Mourik captured a bridge by surprise, overpowering seven or eight German guards. During a subsequent counter-attack at least one German was killed and another seriously wounded, and the NBS fighters held the bridge. This allowed the Royal Canadian Dragoons (RCD – the armoured-car regiment of I Corps) to move northwards undelayed. In total, Van Mourik's group captured 46 German soldiers, and 62 collaborators including LW and WA paramilitaries and NSB members. Only one NBS man died, due to the accidental discharge of a Sten gun after the engagement.

The NBS group in Kollumerland, a municipality in the north-eastern corner of the province, numbered 86 members including two women couriers. This group killed 23 opponents in a series of clashes spread over three days, and lost four of its members in the fighting. The same group

Motorcycle courier Jan Sevinga (compare with Plate G3) carries on his pillion the *Marechaussee* Johannes Kooistra (compare with Plate G1). Both were members of the NBS in the Friesland municipality of Achtkarspelen, where their group captured a bridge at Blauwverlaat to ease the passage of advancing Canadian troops. Kooistra had continued to serve in the police throughout the Occupation, and his apparent cooperation with the German authorities inevitably attracted unjust suspicions about his loyalty. It was only after the Liberation that he received proper credit for his valuable intelligence work for the Resistance. (Courtesy Ieke Jan Sevinga)

(Left) Wearing a British 'pixie' winter tank suit, the Friesland KP leader Piet Oberman – who had carried out a spectacularly successful prison raid in Leeuwarden in December 1944 – rides in a Canadian jeep during the April 1945 liberation of his home town of Dokkum; at this date he commanded the 'sabotage wing' of the Friesland NBS. The jeep is driven by a major in the Royal Canadian Dragoons, the armoured reconnaissance regiment of Canadian I Corps; note the diamond-shaped corps sign below the windscreen. (Beeldbankwo2.nl/ NIOD & Fries Verzetsmuseum)

took a sizeable number of prisoners, variously recorded from 160 to 175 – a motley collection of Orpo, Kriegsmarine, and LW and WA paramilitaries.

In Woudsend, a village in the south-west of the province, a local NBS group numbering only ten to a dozen men (including one German deserter) seized the Welle bridge. This provoked a counter-attack in unexpected strength, by 40–50 Germans supported by an automatic cannon. The NBS squad (whose only Bren gun jammed) was forced to withdraw, permitting the Germans to demolish the bridge. The fighting continued, however, until eventually a Canadian relief force arrived. After two days of fighting, one NBS member and 22 Germans were dead (seven killed by the NBS and 15 by the Canadians).

By 17 April 1945 the province of Friesland was effectively liberated, at a total cost of 32 NBS men killed.

Following the German surrender of 5 May 1945, NBS leaders outside the town hall in Zaanstad, North Holland province, salute together with a Canadian staff officer. The Dutchmen display NBS right-lapel rank patches and 'ORANJE' brassards, the Canadian the sleeve insignia of 21st Army Group. (Courtesy Hanny Kerkhoven)

THE DARK SIDE OF LIBERATION

As the war came to an end the number of NBS recruits increased explosively, and by May 1945 the Netherlands Interior Forces recorded between 150,000 and 200,000 members. Those who joined the NBS shortly before or after the German surrender were mocked as *meikevers* or 'Maybugs' by the veterans of the Resistance, to whom it seemed that suddenly almost everyone in the Netherlands was claiming a part in the struggle.

There were hardly any mechanisms in place to screen this massive influx of newcomers. Consequently, they included not only those with sincere intentions, but also opportunists, criminals, adventurers, and ex-NSB members seeking to whitewash their previous collaboration at this last moment. This had serious consequences for the levels of local discipline among the NBS's swollen membership. Suddenly having in their undisciplined ranks the rogues, the reckless, the vengeful and/or the trigger-happy, the bloated

new NBS would in many cases pose threats to public safety rather than maintaining order. Some of these latecomers were responsible for a number of the summary, extra-judicial revenge-killings which inevitably took place in the immediate aftermath of Liberation. Sadly but inevitably, such episodes dealt a severe blow to the public image and credibility of the NBS as a whole.

One infamous case of public disorder occurred on 7 May 1945 in Amsterdam, two days after the German surrender at Wageningen. There were still plenty of German personnel in the city but few Allied troops, and NBS elements started to disarm and round up both Germans and NSB members, sometimes in the roughest manner. This was in violation of the terms of the surrender agreement, which stipulated that German service personnel

Prince Bernhard (left), the honorary commander-in-chief of the NBS, with Carel Frederik Overhoff, commander of the NBS in Amsterdam. Overhoff's second 'CD' brassard dates the photo to later than 13 May, when it was introduced to identify those members still authorized to bear arms during the sometimes chaotic aftermath of the German surrender (see Plate H8). Prince Bernhard wears British 37-pattern officer's battledress with the rank distinctions of a Dutch lieutenant-general. Note that he displays both the Dutch pilot's brevet on his left breast, and on his right the RAF pilot's 'wings' for which he qualified in autumn 1940. (Rijksmuseum)

The ugly side of the Liberation: a vengeful crowd parades a woman accused of collaboration through the streets of Veenendaal, Utrecht province, in a wheelbarrow. They are led by an NBS man; many (sometimes very recent) members were involved in inflicting humiliating punishments on those perceived to be collaborators, although this was forbidden under the NBS regulations. (Courtesy Martin Brink)

would be disarmed and detained by Allied soldiers, not members of the Resistance. The mounting tensions between nervous parties of Germans and ill-disciplined members of the NBS eventually escalated into shooting around Dam Square, which lasted for about two hours. Tragically, many civilians who were celebrating national liberation got caught in the crossfire, and 32 of them died.

In addition, it was reported that some NBS guards were involved in neglecting, maltreating, and in some cases raping alleged collaborators who were held in temporary internment camps. Examples included incidents at Levantkade camp, Amsterdam; at Harskamp in Gelderland, after Canadian troops handed the guarding of Dutch SS-men over to the ST; and at the former concentration camp at Vught, where *Stoters* were accused of violence against accused collaborators.

The end of the Netherlands Interior Forces

Having outlived their purpose, the NBS were dissolved on 8 August 1945. Some demobilized members resumed their civilian lives, while others opted to serve in other branches of the rebuilt post-war Dutch military. A significant number of NBS veterans volunteered to go to the Dutch East Indies (modern Indonesia), to serve in the counter-insurgency then being waged against Indonesian nationalist insurgents.

H **BRASSARDS**

(1) Netherlands Interior Forces

The plain orange brassard lettered 'ORANJE' in black was the original basic identification for the NBS. It was manufactured in advance in Great Britain, and later in the liberated south of the Netherlands, which produced many minor variations.

(2) NBS, Amsterdam

The most popular type of Dutch-made Resistance brassard proved to be the horizontally striped 'oranje-blanje-bleu' type, made from a light canvas material widely used for sun shades. This material was not judged by the Germans to be suspicious, and so was easily transported through checkpoints. It was then cut and sewn into brassards in secret workshops, and authenticated by the addition of various local stamps. This version, worn in Amsterdam, bears an authentication stamp of the Order Service: 'ORANJE', between two stamps of the city's coat of arms bearing three St Andrew's crosses and flanked by the letters 'O' and 'D'. The 'NBS' overstamp was added later upon the foundation of the unified forces. (From original in Klaas Castelein Collection)

(3) NBS, Delft

This differing example, accidentally cut vertically instead of horizontally, was worn by the NBS in Delft, a city in the western province of South Holland. This bears a black 'OD' authentication stamp, and, faintly visible to the right, the outline of the Dutch heraldic lion. Other overstamping identifies the city (Klaas Castelein Collection).

(4) NBS Combat Wing

This white brassard bears the orange Dutch national lion centred under 'ORANJE' and above 'N.B.S.', and flanked by 'S' and 'G', indicating the wearer's affiliation to the *Strijdend Gedeelte* or 'combat wing' of the Netherlands Interior Forces.

(5) PAN, Eindhoven

This brassard was worn by *Partizanenactie Nederland* members who openly engaged the Germans in the Eindhoven area of North Brabant province in September 1944, at the time of Operation *Market Garden*.

(6) NBS, Heerlen

This brassard was worn by members in the area of Heerlen, a town in southern Limburg province. The brassard bears a blue salamander lizard as an authentication stamp, probably in reference to the regeneration of the Dutch nation (a salamander is reputed to be able to regrow a lost tail). Invisible here on the rear surface of the brassard is an oval-shaped stamp lettered 'ORANJE BRIGADE HEERLEN'.

(7) NBS, The Hague

This brassard was worn by members in The Hague, the national administrative capital located in the western province of South Holland. The black stamp 'BW' overlaying the lettering 'ORANJE' stands for *Burgerwacht* ('Citizen's Guard'). Just visible above the 'W' is a small serial number. Local variations of brassards might feature symbols traditional to their locality; note, faintly at the left, the stork that figures in The Hague's coat-of-arms. (Klaas Castelein Collection)

(8) Civil Defence, May 1945

Immediately following the German surrender on 5 May 1945, fatal shooting incidents occurred between NBS members and German personnel they were attempting to disarm, especially in North and South Holland and Utrecht. This prompted Gen Foulkes, GOC Canadian I Corps, to issue a proclamation on 12 May stating that from 13 May onwards only a limited number of NBS members in those provinces were permitted to carry weapons, and that they were to be identified by British-made black brassards lettered in white 'CD' (for 'Civil Defence').

1

ORANJE

2

ORANJE
N.B.S.

3

4

ORANJE
S G
N.B.S.

5

P A N
Oranje

6

ORANJE

7

BW
05102

8

C D

GLOSSARY AND ABBREVIATIONS

Note: Only Dutch terms are *italicized*.

AA	anti-aircraft
BBO	*Bureau Bijzondere Opdrachten* (Special Assignments Bureau)
BT	*Bewakingstroepen* (Guard Section of BS)
CPN	Communist Party of the Netherlands
CS-6	*Corellistraat 6* (resistance group)
DNB	Dutch National Battalion
Flak	AA artillery (German)
Flakhelfer	AA auxiliary (German}
GLD	Germanischer Landdienst (Germanic Land Service)
GOC	general officer commanding
GV	*Grauwe Vendels* (Grey Banners – paramilitary wing of NF)
HJ	Hitlerjugend (German: Hitler Youth)
HSSPF	Höhere SS- u. Polizeiführer (German: Higher SS & Police Leader)
KK	Kontroll-Kommando (Control Guard)
KL	*Koninklijke Landmacht* (Royal Land Force – Dutch Army)
KP	*knokploeg* (assault team)
Kriegsmarine	German Navy
LKP	*Landelijke Knokploegen* (LO National Assault Teams)
LO	*Landelijke Organisatie voor Hulp aan Onderduikers* (National Organization for Help to People in Hiding)
LSN	*Landstorm Nederland* (Territorial Defence Force)
Luftwaffe	German Air Force
LW	*Landwacht* (Home Guard)
NAD	*Nederlandse Arbeidsdienst* (Netherlands Labour Service)
NBS	*Nederlandse Binnenlandse Strijdkrachten* (Netherlands Interior Forces – not to be confused with NSB)
NF	*Nationaal Front* (National Front)
NJS	*Nationale Jeugdstorm* (National Youth Force)
NSB	*Nationaal-Socialistische Beweging* (National-Socialist Movement – not to be confused with NBS)
NSNAP	*Nationaal Socialistische Nederlandse Arbeiderspartij* (National Socialist Netherlands Workers' Party)
OD	*Ordedienst* (Order Service)
Oostkorps	'East Corps' of RAD
Orpo	Ordnungspolizei (German: Order Police)
OT	Organization Todt (German)
PAN	*Partizanenactie Nederland* (Partisan Action Netherlands)
PoW	prisoner of war
RAD	Reichsarbeitsdienst (German: Reich Labour Service)
RVV	*Raad van Verzet* (Council of Resistance)
SA	Sturmabteilung (German: paramilitary wing of Nazi Party)
SD	Sicherheitsdienst (German: SS Security Service)
SG	*Strijdend Gedeelte* (Combat Wing of NBS)
SHAEF	Supreme Headquarters Allied Expeditionary Force
SK-OT	Schutzkommando-Organization Todt (German)
SOE	Special Operations Executive (British)
ST	*Stoottroepen* (Shock Forces)

Staatspolitie	State Police
WA	*Weerbaarheidsafdeling* (paramilitary wing of NSB)
Wachtmannen	Watchmen
Wehrmacht	German Armed Forces
wolfsangel	'wolf's- hook' runic symbol
ZF	*Zwart Front* (Black Front)
ZS	*Zwarte Storm* (Black Force)

Present-day commemorative ceremony in Haarlem honouring the executed heroine Hannie Schaft, and paying tribute to all the other women who served in the Resistance. The sculpture was made after the war by Truus Menger-Oversteegen, Schaft's former comrade in the Haarlem RVV. Here NBS re-enactors form a guard of honour, wearing black-painted helmets and blue overalls and carrying Sten guns. (Courtesy W.C. Brand)

SELECT BIBLIOGRAPHY

Books
Note: The titles mentioned below are the main studies that have been consulted. Other useful books, focusing on sub-topics, are not listed here.

Afiero, Massimiliano, *Dutch Waffen-SS Legion & Brigade 1941–44*, MAA 531 (Osprey Publishing; Oxford, 2020)

Bouchery, Jean, *The British Soldier, from D-Day to VE-Day* (Histoire & Collections; Paris, 2012)

Breen, Willem F. van, *De Nederlandsche Arbeidsdienst 1940–1945, Ontstaan, opkomst en ondergang* (Walburg Pers; Zutphen, 2004)

Buitkamp, J., *Geschiedenis van het verzet 1940–1945* (Bibula/Unieboek; Houten, 1990)